Excursion for Miracles

Excursion for Miracles

Paul Sanasardo, Donya Feuer, and

Studio for Dance, 1955–1964

Mark Franko

Wesleyan University Press   Middletown, Connecticut

Published by Wesleyan University Press,
Middletown, CT 06459
www.wesleyan.edu/wespress
© 2005 by Mark Franko
All rights reserved

ISBN 0-8195-6743-4 cloth
ISBN 0-8195-6744-2 paper

Cover photo: Paul Sanasardo and Donya Feuer in a
    studio portrait (1962). Photo: Zachary Freyman.
Frontispiece: Donya Feuer in *In View of God* (1960).
    Photo: Stephen Balkin.
Printed in the United States of America
Designed and typeset in Cycles, Flemish Script, and
    Futura Condensed by Julie Allred, BW&A Books,
    Inc., Durham, N.C.

5   4   3   2   1

Cataloging-in-Publication Data appear on the last
printed page of this book

For Danny, who clung tightly to Paul's back and
who always said "When I grow up and you grow down".

Daniel Leon Canner

(December 8, 1950–September 13, 2004)

People work much in order to secure the future;
I gave my mind much work and trouble, trying to secure the past.

—*Isak Dinesen,* Shadows on the Grass

Contents

Illustrations

Preface

*There is no critique which is not immanent and
already real and material before it is conscious.*
—Louis Althusser, "The Piccolo Teatro"

In 1964, at the age of eighteen, I began to study dance with Paul Sanasardo after seeing *Laughter after All,* a revised version of the work that
he originally choreographed with Donya Feuer in 1960. Shortly after
my coming to the studio, Judith Blackstone, a dancer in his company
and my school friend at the High School of Performing Arts, asked me
to dance a duet with her, *Broken Voyage.* Judith had been dancing with
Paul and Donya from the time she was eleven years old. She invited
Paul to see her choreography in an informal studio showing. I now realize that *Broken Voyage* was reminiscent of Feuer's *Dust for Sparrows,* the
duet that Donya had made for herself and Judith and that had initiated their large-scale works for children. Judith's choreography introduced me as a novice to Paul; he invited me to join the company
shortly thereafter.

In the first piece of choreography that Paul created "on me"—a
short solo in *An Earthly Distance* (1966)—I rolled out of the fabric that
Donya had used in the birth scene of *Excursion for Miracles.* The fabric
still contained the scent of Donya's perfume. In the next few years, be-
sides dancing in many new works, I was performing in revivals of some

Mark Franko and Judith Blackstone in Blackstone's *Broken Voyage* (1966). Photo: Charlotte Victoria.

of the older ones. To me everything was linked to what had come before, including the experience of the children.

Excursion for Miracles focuses on the body of choreographic work that Paul Sanasardo and Donya Feuer created in the late fifties and early sixties. As the first attempt to discuss their collaboration, it shifts emphasis from Judson Dance Theatre as the only site of choreographic innovation for that period.[1] Since I performed with the Paul Sanasardo Dance Company from 1964 until 1969, this is also a personal book. I recall their work from diverse perspectives: recreating it with the help of archival documents and also sensing it with the dancer's kinesthetic recall. I interpret its meanings today, however, in ways I then only sensed. To reveal the critical and the artistic import of Sanasardo and Feuer's work has meant for me both a radical return to my own adolescent experience and a radical distancing from it. I am combining

Donya Feuer in the early sixties.

the critical theory that I have developed as a dance scholar with an ethnographic approach to the material that includes myself as informant.

My personal involvement in this history has convinced me of the need for oral testimony and the value of it. Because this work has never taken its place in dance history, an archive had to be assembled, but also in a sense created, before this book could be written. This effort has succeeded because of the enormous generosity of all who participated. There are many voices here, although I am sure that there could have been more. (Apologies to potential contributors that I could not locate.) The result is neither biography nor autobiography, nor history in the conventional sense, although it might be a step toward a microhistory of one important dance company.[2]

This may have something to do with the archive itself as a repository of feelings and impressions more than of facts, dates, and the like.

> This is a history carried by many people. They continue it and live within it.
>
> —Donya Feuer

Fragments of earlier discourses—transformed over time—become recognizable as they are voiced again. This archive is vivid and seems almost to erase the passage of time. It was in the very nature of the Sanasardo-Feuer collaboration to spark feelings directly from dance. This archive collects and exhibits *intensities* and remains true in this way to the dances to which they are testimonials.

"Intensity" is a word that springs from the lips of all whom I interviewed. But it is a difficult concept to describe. Richard Schechner and Willa Appel describe "intensity of performance" as the moment when "a certain threshold is crossed—that moment when spectators and performers alike sense a 'successful' performance is taking place." "In this sense," they continue, "intensity can be likened to 'flow,' 'concentration' and 'presence.'"[3] Intensity is frequently also understood as the performer's ability to "fill" the performance with expressive meaning.

These definitions are helpful and revealing, but I should like to consider another possible meaning of intensity that places greater significance in the concept of crossing a threshold. Intensity can also move us beyond the fulfillment of performance's skills and codes toward a breaching of the systems of meaning (social, linguistic, conventional) in which they find themselves embedded. Intensity is indeed a crossing of the threshold in that it can confront us with "untamed" areas of experience, what José Gil calls a "kind of methodological breakout" from "the domain marked out by signs."[4] The very same term is both the lingua franca of the ethnographic account and the theoretical term central to my interpretation.

Many of the photographs reproduced here capture and freeze this breakout. They are for the most part unposed "action" shots taken from the stage wings or in the studio. One could almost say that they bridge a crucial gap—almost a "time-lapse" operation—between performance, its recollection, and subsequent interpretation. The photographs are talismans of intensities because their very status as evidence hovers between the personal, the documentary, and the artistic. They manifest presence, absence, and lines of flight all at once. This multiple role accounts to some degree for their emotional charge.

The project of recovering these intensities and representing them in writing becomes problematic if one believes that experience itself is by definition unrecoverable. Perhaps for this reason, the visual artist Frank Stella has faulted criticism for always seeking a context for in-

Paul Sanasardo in the early sixties.

terpretation.[5] Stella proposed that the context of the artist is the time it takes to create the work itself. He speaks for a particular sensibility of his generation. "Choreographing a work is such an immediate process," Sanasardo has remarked, "and the situation and the place in time with the dancers in the studio are the forces that most shape the work."[6] This methodology is in part what has precluded their art from memory. Can any sort of verbal representation model itself on this immediacy without falling into the trap of formalism? If context is limited to the moment of art's creation, then interpretation is necessarily a betrayal, because it comes afterward, a point made famously by Susan Sontag in *Against Interpretation*.[7] Still, the separation of art from all discursively interpretive practices can result in a critical formalism —or at best in subtle paraphrases—out of keeping with this material. For the intensities also called forth—paradoxically—a sense of removal that distinguished early postmodern dance from both expressionism and from conceptual art.

Stella does not call for a formalist criticism, and such a procedure would be unsuitable to the work of Sanasardo and Feuer. The thread connecting Stella, Sontag, and Sanasardo and Feuer is that of a nominalism, by which I mean a healthy respect for the singularity of the event. Philip Auslander has described radical avant-garde theater of the sixties as being imbued with "presence" and "liveness," two qualities it also shared with the postmodern dance of that time.[8] But I propose the decisive quality of the dance to be "intensities," suggesting it as a more plastic term than "liveness." The event's singularity is conveyed as such by its intensities.

Sanasardo and Feuer's work brought together the autobiographical with pop eclecticism, dance with theatricality, poetry with social critique (at the immanent and material level, as Althusser says), intellectualism with "experience," intensities with rigorous stagecraft. This heterogeneity is itself the antithesis of formalism, so it is useful to remember that while interpretation for Sontag was content examined, the actual benefit to be accrued from the rejection of interpretation was "to experience more immediately what we have."[9] The question is whether immediacy is the appropriate term for this fullness of experience. Let us ponder again Althusser's thought: the quality of critique is immanent, real, and material before it is conscious. I propose intensity, or *intensities,* because they underline the materiality of experience as such. Yet they can also be curiously *mediating* as well as stunningly *visceral.* They are the nascent form of critique. Intensity has the capacity to call forth the opposite of immediacy: the distancing that fosters critique. Its power is to reveal a "disalienating" activity, that is, an activity that alienates us from alienation.

As is by now clear, many critical terms that I use here—externality, singularity, event, intensities—are taken from contemporary poststructuralist thought, especially from Jean-François Lyotard's and Gilles Deleuze's writings on aesthetics and art. Rainer Maria Rilke, however, used the term "event" much earlier. Issues of alienation, conformity, and individualism were prevalent in American sociology of the fifties and sixties (Mills, Riesman, Whyte) and also hark back to the post-Marxian Frankfurt school tradition (notably to Lukács) that found new life in the United States through Herbert Marcuse in the sixties. Methodologically, I am bringing early postmodern dance, Frankfurt school theory, American sociology, and poststructuralist theory together with personal memories. I am, however, not presenting contemporary thought relevant to the choreography as *applied to* it or *illustrated by* it. While the Sanasardo-Feuer work is contemporaneous with some concerns of Riesman and Marcuse, the question is not one of pinpointing those influences as such. Most strikingly Sanasardo and Feuer's work precedes poststructuralist thought.

The ideas that form this book first germinated forty years ago, on a February evening in 1964, when I saw *Laughter after All,* the work that best illustrates what I mean by intensities. Chapter 2 is a report on that evening. The works for the children are grouped in chapter 3. Chapter 4 is devoted to *Excursion for Miracles,* and chapter 5 returns to *Laughter after All* for an extended analysis.

Excursion for Miracles introduces not only forgotten choreographic work but also the embodiment of an unthought idea. This book claims an unrecognized, *material* occasion of poststructural critique for early postmodern dance.[10] Dance history and critical theory break away from any hierarchical or precoded relationship between practice and theory, and the ethnographic aspect of this study supports this break.

San Francisco
August 2004

Acknowledgments

A child of happy circumstance, this book was made possible by my nine years of discussions with many people by phone, letter, and best of all in person in New York City, Stockholm, San Francisco, Paris, and Amsterdam, and at the farm in Cooperstown, New York. Were it not for the extreme generosity of Paul Sanasardo, Donya Feuer, and all the dancers I was able to find (see the biographical notes of informants at the end of this book), I could not have completed this project. I am especially appreciative of the time that Pina Bausch afforded Paul, Donya, and me in her dressing room at the Brooklyn Academy of Music in October, 2001, to discuss her work with them. Interviews with Robert Natkin, Sally Bowden, Jacques Patarozzi, and Anneliese Widman were also extremely valuable.

The Getty Center for the History of Art and the Humanities generously supported early stages of this work during my residence there between 1994 and 1995. I am grateful to the Committee on Research at the University of California, Santa Cruz, for providing a special research grant just when it was most needed. I completed the writing with a grant from the American Council of Learned Societies, and I cannot express sufficient gratitude for that support.

I presented a version of chapter 3 at the Performance Studies Formations Conference (Northwestern University, 1996), and at the conference "Sous le double signe de l'effacement et du possible: la danse contemporaine au détour du siècle" (Le Mas de la Danse, Fontvieille, 2000), by the invitation of Dominique and Françoise Dupuy. An early version of chapter 4 was read at the International Conference "Dancing in the Millennium" (Washington, D.C., 2000). I thank Gay Morris for editing an earlier version of my discussion of *Laughter after All* for her anthology *Moving Words: Re-writing Dance*. A different version of my analysis of Paul Taylor's *Seven New Dances* appeared in *ballettanz* (2003). I would like to express my thanks to Christina Caprioli for inviting Donya, Paul, and myself to discuss their work in a public forum at the "Movement Is a Woman" dance festival (Stockholm, October, 2000). Finally, I am most appreciative of the advice, critical input, and collegial support of Peter Bohlin, Claudia Gabler, Damara Vita Ganley, David Gere, Maria Holm, Marc Jampole, Rebekah Kowal, André Lepecki, Laurence Louppe, Debra McCall, Randy Martin, Dick McCaw, Armando Menicacci, Jean Rochereau, Janice Ross, Suzanna Tamminen, Constance Vallis Hill, and Myriam Van Imschoot.

Last but not least, many thanks are due the librarians and archivists of the Dance Collection at the Lincoln Center Library for the Performing Arts, the Dansmuseet, the Sveriges Teatermuseum, and the Paul Taylor Dance Foundation Archives.

51 West 19th Street

Dancing is a human possibility.
—*Donya Feuer*

As choreographic, pedagogical, and stage partners from 1955 until 1963, Paul Sanasardo and Donya Feuer collaborated on four important evening-length works, among other things. Those works, *In View of God* (1959), *Laughter after All* (1960 and 1964), *Excursion for Miracles* (1961), and *Pictures in Our House* (1961), are the main subjects of this book.[1] Created in the short space of three years, between 1959 and 1961, they are early examples of the evening-length modern dance. They combined elements of popular culture, classical ballet, and theater in modern dance before it was fashionable to do so and constructed the works from layers of poetic insight, autobiography, and psychodrama. Sanasardo and Feuer also trained a handful of extremely talented children, integrating them into their dances to evocative effect.[2] Without programmatic signposts or agitprop tendencies, their work conveyed social, political, and religious significance.

But perhaps collaboration itself is the most novel feature of their work. In comparison to other sixties collaborators working across different media, the Sanasardo-Feuer collaboration was uniquely all within one medium—the only instance I am aware of in which two choreographers "signed" the same works.[3] Their collaboration could be said to destabilize choreographic authorship, not by reducing or eliminating personal intention, as in the case of Cunningham and Cage, but by multiplying it. Some of their dances were occasions of intensive accumulation, suggesting the abundance of pop art rather than the minimalism generally associated with sixties postmodern dance. Sanasardo and Feuer prefigure aspects of the Tanztheater of Pina Bausch, who worked with them when she first came to America at age eighteen. Their work, like that of Bausch, was intricately autobiographical and surrealistic.

Setting the Stage

When Sanasardo and Feuer met in 1954, he was a scholarship student in Martha Graham's professional class. Originally from Chicago, he came to New York directly after his military service in Washington, D.C. Feuer was born and raised in Philadelphia. She came to Graham's studio via the Juilliard School and was being groomed for the company.[4] The 1955 premiere of Anna Sokolow's *Rooms,* which upset the dance world with its stark social realism and unusual use of a jazz score, catalyzed their relationship.[5] Sanasardo's performance in *Rooms,* which Feuer saw at its premiere, generated a violent discussion between them and was the beginning of their collaboration. Shortly thereafter Feuer choreographed a duet to celebrate their friendship, *I'll Be You and You Be Me.*[6]

In October 1955 Feuer left New York with Graham on a tour sponsored by the State Department to Southeast Asia, and Sanasardo joined the Broadway cast of Sean O'Casey's *Red Roses for Me,* choreographed by Anna Sokolow.[7] Although neither would return to the Graham studio, this separation was only a temporary parting of the ways, since they had already decided to work together. In 1956 they shared a concert with Paul Taylor and Anneliese Widman at the Master Institute Theater in upper Manhattan (June 5, 1956).[8] In 1957 Sanasardo and Feuer formed the Contemporary Theater of Dance-Drama-Music to support interdisciplinary choreography integrating the spoken word (Gertrude Stein and Virginia Woolf), original musical composition (Charles Wuorinen and David Johnson), and visual art (David and Sylvia Lund). A fund-raising letter sought to attract eight hundred

DANCE - DRAMA - MUSIC

presents

A SERIOUS DANCE FOR 3 FOOLS

Choreography:...Donya Feuer

Music: David Johnson

Sets executed by: David, Sylvia Lund

Excerpts from Virginia Woolf

WORDS FOR CONVERSATION

FACADE .... Donya Feuer, Anneliese Widman,
Paul Sanasardo

    FANTASY .... Danya Feuer

    LANDSCAPE .... Paul Sanasardo

    STILL LIFE .... Anneliese Widman, Paul Sanasardo

ECLIPSE .... Donya Feuer, Anneliese Widman,
Paul Sanasardo

"Yet there are moments when the walls of the mind grow thin; when nothing is unabsorbed, and I could fancy
that we might blow so vast a bubble that the sun might set and rise in it and we might take the blue of midday
and the black of midnight and be cast off and escape from here and now."

VIRGINIA WOOLF

intermission

A Dance Adaption of
Gertrude Stein's

"DOCTOR FAUSTUS LIGHTS THE LIGHTS"

Production Designed and Directed by Paul Sanasardo
Music: Charles Wuorinen

    FAUSTUS .... Paul Sanasardo

    MARGUERITE IDA AND HELENA ANNABEL .... Donya Feuer

    WOMAN .... Ellen Green

In this adaption of Stein's Doctor Faustus I have hoped to present not a classical Faust image but rather that
of a man who regrets the loss of love through the contrivances of his own vanity.

Credits: Conductor, Leon Hyman; Musicians, Martha Blackman, Richard Koff, Morris Newman,
Douglas Nordley, Howard Van Hyning, Charles Russo; Lighting, Nicola Cernovich; Costumes,
Ursula Reed.

The program for *Dance-Drama-Music* (1957).

dollars for the production of Sanasardo's *A Dance Adaptation of Gertrude Stein's "Doctor Faustus Lights the Lights"* and Feuer's *A Serious Dance for Three Fools*.[9] The choreographers wrote, "Fully realizing that we are not a recognized and established group, we have tried to be direct and explicit in this letter, and make this request on the strength of our eagerness to dare this venture." Although they authored these dances separately, each dancer figured prominently in the other's work.[10] That summer Sanasardo and Feuer directed the dance program at a children's summer camp run by F. Jacobs in Indian Head, Pennsylvania. Their earnings financed the renovation of three lofts they had found on 19th Street between Fifth and Sixth Avenues, at 51 West 19th Street, on the outskirts of Manhattan's garment district in Chelsea.

Studio for Dance

Studio for Dance occupied the three lofts on 19th Street, which it rented for a total of $250 monthly. Sanasardo and Feuer's collaboration was characterized by closely shared working and living conditions: the property became their base of operations and their home. A walled-off corner of the largest fourth-floor studio became Feuer's living quarters. The third floor of the building was used for dressing rooms, a costume shop, a storage space for sets, and an art gallery. The smaller second-floor studio doubled as an apartment for Sanasardo and Bill Weaver, the actor–stage manager who discreetly and elegantly stage-managed the creative disorder of their lives. On the ground floor of Studio for Dance's building was a cardboard box manufacturer. The fire escape in the rear led to the neighboring building, where weekend jazz parties were held. One of the studio's neighbors was the African-American musician Wilbur de Paris, who occasionally on his way home stopped in to drum for classes. Sanasardo and Feuer team-taught the first class at Studio for Dance, then pooled their earnings to have dinner a few blocks downtown in Greenwich Village.

One of the early pop art shows held at Studio for Dance in 1961 dis-

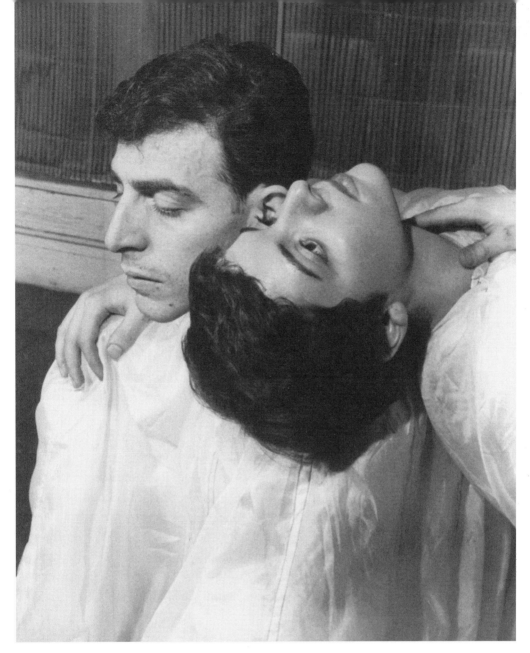

Paul Sanasardo and Donya Feuer in Feuer's *A Serious Dance for Three Fools* (1957).

played work by Stephan Durkee, Robert Indiana, and Richard Smith. A domino sculpture by Indiana graced the first-floor landing for years after. The unnamed *Art News* reviewer commented that "these artists must feel that art is not very far from life."[11] The same could also be said of Sanasardo and Feuer's choreography, as mirrored in the environment they fashioned for themselves on 19th Street. "Home and work," remarks Feuer, "were in the same place. Everything was possible because we were available to each other." This kind of close connection between art practices and everyday life has become almost impossible to achieve today with the increasing loss of privacy and individuality at the sites of collective creativity. "Manhattan in the fifties," remembers Sanasardo, "was still rather an innocent place, and remarkably affordable for young artists. Because of the impropriety of living in a loft—which was somewhat illegal—it was possible to have a unique setup, even if it had to be somewhat hidden."

The neighborhood of Studio for Dance was bustling during working hours. But after dark it was deserted, resembling what Jane Jacobs was to describe in 1961 as the "border vacuums" of American cities: "the edge of an area of 'ordinary' city."[12] This edge was indeed extraordinary. It was an urban no-man's-land between "uptown" and "downtown," legitimate theater and bohemianism, the established and experimental dance worlds of the city, which were also identified as uptown and downtown. In some ways, the work of Sanasardo and Feuer, set between the legitimate and the experimental, occupied an analogous position on the map of New York City dance. Historically, the neighborhood contained traces of the former Broadway theater district (around Madison Square Park) and the department stores that were subsequently transferred to 34th Street.[13] Accounts of the sixties avant-garde associate dance experimentalism with Greenwich Village, but this version of the urban topography of avant-garde dance omits the garment district, which might be extended to include 14th Street and Canal Street, their preferred source of materials for sets and costumes. These were working-class neighborhoods without the patina of a bohemian past.

Without grants or special patronage, Sanasardo and Feuer developed their own company of child and adult dancers. Among the company's gifted young dancers at that time was Pina Bausch.[14] Bausch, Sanasardo, and Feuer became lasting friends during their work together in 1959 and 1960. Bausch took over the wife/mother role in the second performance of *In View of God*. The only three-way collaboration undertaken by Sanasardo and Feuer was with Bausch. They choreographed *Phases of Madness* together, a trio that implied a triangle in behavioral if not narrative terms, danced to Varèse's *Octandre*.[15] *Phases* was performed eight times in the winter and spring of 1960 with Arthur Weisberg's Contemporary Chamber Ensemble on a tour of city schools sponsored by the Neighborhood Committee for the Arts of the Upper West Side.[16]

Phases of Madness was significant for its premise of "dancing madness"—the idea that certain behaviors exceed the bounds of rationality and are most readily conveyed by dancing. A full insight into people had to encompass this unsettling dimension.[17] Sanasardo, Feuer, and Bausch came to their understanding of madness through personal encounters. In other words, they danced madness not as a clinical condition, as had German modern dancer Harald Kreutzberg in his *Irre Gestalten* (*Mad Figures*), but as a way of living outside the system.[18] The freedom Sanasardo and Feuer experienced as young artists in their studio-home, a freedom contagious to those around them, came with high emotional tension. Above all, madness was relative: it was a product of social interaction, not an individualized symptom. To be free to be mad charged the atmosphere.[19] The conditions of the studio were in a sense more those of the stage than those of everyday life. This was not an environment to be engaged with casually. One either liked it or one did not.

In *Phases of Madness*, Feuer, Bausch, and Sanasardo each performed one of madness's phases, the totality of which lay beyond any one individual. Madness existed in the encounter. They understood madness both as a condition of contemporary society and as a possibility of their work. Madness indicates a situation or state of being that is fraught with both potential and danger. Sanasardo returned to the implications of "socialized"

It was Mr. Tudor who introduced Pina Bausch to us and made the suggestion that it might be to our advantage to ask Pina to work with us. It was not difficult to recognize Pina's exceptional talent. Pina could not say much in English, and Donya and I had no knowledge of German, but we could dance together in a very special way.
—Paul Sanasardo

I only know that if I had never met you I think everything would have been different. I found some friends forever. It was really important in my life and I don't know exactly why. But I think that we found each other, and it was something forever. It's very funny but I cannot tell you why, exactly why it was so important. I only *know* it, we know it all together.
—Pina Bausch speaking to Feuer and Sanasardo

She [Pina] had an agreement with gravity; it didn't pull her down. She went to gravity.
—Donya Feuer

(at center L to R) Donya Feuer, Paul Sanasardo, and Pina Bausch in a curtain call for *Phases of Madness* (1960). Photo: V. Sladon.

I always felt free. And I felt no one could judge me, and if they judged me it didn't matter. I am gone, I am here, I am off the stage, I am on. They were a captive audience, and whatever I presented was accepted. And in real life you can't just present anything, you can't be just the way you wish to be. Someone's feelings might be hurt, you might speak too boldly, or you might not say the right thing. But on the stage you can just be. Whatever you're supposed to do, you can do it totally.

—Chifra Holt

madness in *Pain* (1969); Feuer did so in her production of Lars Noren's *Fursteslickaren* (*The Prince's Asslicker*) (1973); and Bausch, in *Blaubart* (*Bluebeard*) (1977). *Phases of Madness* also contained the kernel of the evening-length *Laughter after All* (1960), which Bausch may have rehearsed but did not ultimately perform.

By the mid-sixties the child dancers, who had first arrived in 1957, were nearing puberty and began to join the adult ranks of the dance company. Judith Blackstone, Willa Kahn, Judith Canner Moss, and Ellen Shookoff, in particular, took on mature roles by the 1963–1964 season. This was still a very precocious company, however, and the haunting quality of its work in the early sixties owed something to the provocative ambiguities between childhood and adulthood that it suggested. I discuss *In View of God* and *Pictures in Our House*, two works created expressly for the children, in chapter 3. Feuer's *Dust for Sparrows* (1958) pointed the way to *In View of God* and was seminal for the roles that children came to play.

The final scene of Feuer's *Fursteslickaren* (*The Prince's Asslicker*) at the Dramaten (Stockholm, 1975). Photo: Beata Bergström.

From the beginning, New York dance critics regularly reviewed Studio for Dance concerts.[20] The company had a small, loyal following for its appearances at Hunter Playhouse, the Henry Street Settlement House, and the 92nd Street Y, which was one of the most important venues at that time for modern dance.[21]

Modern dancers in the 1960s were frequently trained by a choreographer rather than by a dance teacher. The integration of particular artistic criteria into technical training enabled dancers to infuse the choreographer's vision with their own identities as artists and as people, and their particular ways of moving could in turn affect the choreographic vision.

Small modern dance companies in the 1960s tended to be closely knit "micro-groups."[22] A shared vision inspired by the choreographer,

I felt they knew something
about me.

—Diane Germaine

He liked to think of himself as a
father, but he really wasn't. He was
more of a keeper: he didn't want
anyone to stray. For some people
it was too much, and they had to
get out.

—Regina Axelrod

and resulting personal affinities between choreographer and dancer, held companies together in the absence of paychecks. Since the economic basis of most small companies was shaky at best, they were sustained by personal will and dogged persistence. A choreographer-led school could support the company artistically, morally, and financially. The choreographer-teacher jealously guarded his or her profession of intent, iconoclastic mission, and disdain for commercialism. Corporate and foundation support was virtually unheard of, and the National Endowment for the Arts did not yet exist.

Dancer training and choreographic creativity were interconnected. Dancers were often trained to execute in class the very material that they performed on stage, thus skipping the step between classroom training and repertory. Among those who would affect Studio for Dance's style and direction were Loretta Abbott, Manuel Alum, Diane Germaine, and Joan Lombardi, all of whom found their way to the studio during the sixties.

The company was diverse for the period: Alum was born in Arecibo, Puerto Rico, and was to emerge in the mid-sixties as a choreographer of note.[23] Among the African American dancers performing with the company were Loretta Abbott, Gus Solomons Jr., Diana Ramos, Strody Meekins, Martin Bland, and guest artist Miguel Godreau.

It was possible to survive in New York even without much money, and the relative penury of choreographers, dancers, designers, and some audiences alike was not necessarily limiting. There was, moreover, what Feuer calls "the need for the intensity of it all." Concerts were prepared as much as one year in advance of their premiere but were often performed only once. The dearth of performances supported Feuer and Sanasardo's singularity by concentrating everyone's effort on one event. Studio for Dance productions were personal and poetic, as well as provocative and disturbing.

Rupture and Continuities

The Sanasardo-Feuer collaboration came to an unexpected end in February 1963, when Feuer left New York for Sweden to teach and choreograph at the Swedish Ballet Akademian (Ballet Academy) in Stock-

holm.[24] By this time the delicate balance of the collaborative relationship had been deteriorating. Because of growing tensions, very little of
the final collaboration, *Of Human Kindness,* is documented, a problem
further compounded by the absence of photographs. Looking back on
it, Sanasardo feels that they had been trying to soften the pessimism of
their work until then. *Of Human Kindness* featured exuberant movement, which made it agreeable to watch, with an original score and
live orchestra under the direction of composer Edwin Finckel. The
work examined aspects of love by seeking a balance between inno-
cence and experience, the two extreme poles of Feuer and Sanasardo's
work. But a mystery surrounds the final duet between Sanasardo and
Feuer, "The Eternal Affair," which Walter Sorell called "a cold flirta-
tion" and found shockingly "unkind."[25] Until the final duet, loving is
painful but lyrical; but in that duet, another tone emerges, an ambiguity, which seems cold and cruel. The title therefore is ironic, even bit-
ter, suggesting that cruelty, not kindness, is inherent to the species.

Feuer left for Sweden several days after *Of Human Kindness* was performed. She has lived ever since in Stockholm, where she joined the
Kungliga Dramatiska Teatern (Royal Dramatic Theater, also known as
the Dramaten), first as choreographer (1966) and then
a year later, at the invitation of Ingmar Bergman and
Erland Josephson, as director. By collaborating with Alf
Sjöberg, Frank Sundström, and Bergman, Feuer's own
work as a choreographer and stage director has become
intimately linked with the rich theatrical tradition of
the Dramaten. In 1964 Bergman presented *Hjärtat &
revbenet* (*The Heart and the Rib*), a production that brought
Feuer's choreography together with Ulf Björlin's music
and the sets and costumes of Lennart Mörk, thus pre-
cipitating a greater collaboration between dance, theater, and music at the Dramaten. In 1971 Feuer formed
Dans Kompaniet (Dance Company), which became the
vehicle for her choreography through 1976. As a choreographer for theater Feuer's groundbreaking work has
been influential for the contemporary European practice of mise-en-scène. She has concerned herself not only
with dance but also with the movements of stage actors.
This work, and her close collaboration with directors,
notably Ingmar Bergman, has delineated a new space of

> We explored pain, romanticism, sex-
> uality, but also something that keeps
> going, that's been there all the time
> and keeps people together—the
> affair that is ongoing and profound.
> —Paul Sanasardo

> The Swedish trip was worked out
> before we got onstage, and it surely
> affected what we did onstage. More
> than we knew was playing out in
> *Of Human Kindness.* It was a way
> of parting.
> —Donya Feuer

Pina Bausch in *Philips 836887DSY* (Saratoga, 1971).

scenic creativity. Both in her choreography and her film she has continued to probe the borders between acting and dancing.[26]

After Feuer's departure Sanasardo assumed sole direction of the company and school. In 1963 the Paul Sanasardo Dance Company toured the Midwest, and by 1967 it had developed into a mobile ensemble of eight or so dancers, traveling with sets and costumes. One of Sanasardo's signal creations was this "second" company, which he had personally trained and which matured between 1969 and 1972.[27] It was most impressively showcased in two of his acclaimed works set to the music of contemporary Polish composers: *Cut Flowers* (Kazimierz Serocki, 1966) and *Pain* (Witold Lutowslewski, 1969).

Not all traces of the first company disappeared. Many of the child performers, now grown up, continued to work in Sanasardo's company. In the early seventies there were also new transcontinental interactions between Sanasardo, Feuer, and Bausch. Feuer returned to New York in 1971 to teach the company *Gud lever och har hälsan* (*God Is Alive and in Fairly Good Health*) (1971). Likewise, Bausch returned in 1972 to perform *Philips 836887 DSY* (1971) and to stage *Nachnull* (*Afterzero*) (1970). All three ballets were performed during the company's summer residencies at the Saratoga Performing Arts Center in Saratoga Springs, New York, where Sanasardo was in charge of the School of Modern Dance and Theater of Modern Dance between 1969 and 1974 at Spa Summer Theatre. In 1971 Manuel Alum, a virtuoso but also extremely personal dancer, performed in Feuer's *Spel för museet* (*A Play for a Museum*) (1966), set in the Hall of Runes of Stockholm's Historiska Museet (Historical Museum).[28] Feuer invited Diane Germaine to dance in the Stockholm premiere of *Varg rop* (*The Howling of Wolves*) (1971), also performed amid the runes.

Malou Airaudo and Dominique Mercy, who originally came to New York from Angers, France, to work with Alum, met Bausch in Saratoga in 1972. In 1973 they became founding members of the Wuppertaler Tanztheater (Wuppertal Dance Theatre) in Germany. For Bausch, "It was like a family, the same family." Sanasardo dancer Jacques Patarozzi also later danced for Bausch. These continued interactions signal a continuity of interests and a community of friendship and influence.

In the early seventies most of Sanasardo's company was French, with Michelle Rebeaud, Dominique Petit, Christine Varjan, and Jacques Patarozzi dancing with the troupe, and Airaudo and Mercy joining for shorter periods. Patarozzi and Petit subsequently became well-known performers, choreographers, and teachers in France, which suggests Sanasardo's influence on French modern dance. His European presence had grown by the mid-seventies, when he received choreographic commissions from ballet and modern companies in France and Portugal.[29] From 1977 until 1980 Sanasardo lived in Tel Aviv, where he directed the Batsheva Dance Company, creating six works that were performed both in Israel and internationally. During this time Feuer choreographed and directed in Norway and the Netherlands, in addition to working in Sweden. As of 2004 she has completed five dance films. Both artists have thus contributed greatly to the dance culture in Europe, the Middle East, and North America.[30]

In 1963 Studio for Dance moved a few blocks north of its original location to 59 West 21st Street. It remained open until 1989, when the building was sold. On his return from Israel, Sanasardo reestablished his company in New York, where his work continued to be seen regularly until 1986. He subsequently moved to Cooperstown, New York, and now lives in Chicago.[31] Feuer is active in theater and film in Stock-

holm; her most recent production with Bergman was Schiller's *Maria Stuarda* (2000).

It is evident from this condensed synopsis of the aftermath of the Sanasardo-Feuer collaboration that one book cannot do justice to the nomadic life work of these artists. For this reason I limit myself here to the origins of their work in the late fifties and early sixties.

Backgrounds and Influences

Donya Feuer was born in Philadelphia, Pennsylvania, on October 31, 1934. Her father, Samuel Kasakoff, of Russian Jewish origin, was a chemist and photographer who had immigrated to North Carolina. Her mother, Pauline Feuer, was an internationally known social worker who was called in for questioning by the Eastman Committee (the New Orleans branch of the House un-American Activities Committee) in the early fifties.

Feuer studied dance from the age of seven at the Settlement Music School of Philadelphia under Nadia Chilkovsky, who was an important figure in the left-wing modern dance movement in the 1930s.[32] Feuer performed with Chilkovsky's Philadelphia Children's Dance Theatre until 1950.[33] For Feuer it was an extremely comprehensive and intense training period. Chilkovsky pioneered the use of Laban movement analysis and Labanotation in children's dance training. Musical education and improvisation were included in this schooling, which Chilkovsky ultimately integrated into the Philadelphia public school curriculum. When Feuer was fifteen, her family moved to Detroit and from there to New Orleans. By 1952 Feuer was a scholarship student at the Juilliard School. After a year and a half, however, she left Juilliard to understudy roles and apprentice with the Martha Graham Dance Company. She also danced with Natanya Neumann and Paul Taylor.

Feuer credits Martha Graham as the major inspiration in her dance career. She acknowledged her debt to Graham again recently, in the film *Martha Graham 100 AR: En födelsedagshalsning av Donya Feuer* (*Martha Graham's 100th Year: A Personal Birthday Greeting by Donya Feuer*). Feuer made the film expressly for broadcast on Swedish television on May 11,

facing: Manuel Alum and Karin Thulin in Feuer's *A Play for a Museum,* Stockholm, 1966. Photo: Beata Bergström.

1994, the day Graham would have been one hundred years old, had she lived that long. It is a very personal remembrance—Feuer calls it "art for occasions"—that begins with Feuer perusing the Barbara Morgan book of Graham photographs, with Aaron Copland's *Appalachian Spring* playing in the background, while she recalls the book's impact on her childhood. "For me," notes Feuer, "art for occasions is one of the best ways you can thank people for daring to do what they did."

Paul Sanasardo was born in Chicago on September 15, 1928, to Frances and Joseph Sanasardo. He was brought up on Chicago's South Side in a working-class Sicilian family. The theatrical quality of much of Roman Catholicism looms large in his background. Paolo Franco Vicenzo Giuseppe Sanasardo held fast to his first-generation Italian American identity by resisting Graham's advice to anglicize his surname as well as resisting the trend among pop artists to adopt American place names as personal names (Robert Indiana suggested he change his name to Paul Chicago).[34]

Between 1947 and 1951 Sanasardo studied painting and set design at the Chicago Art Institute under Bauhaus artist Paul Weighardt. Weighardt emphasized process over product, and the distinction between fine and commercial art. He encouraged his students to paint over "finished" work and to seek new solutions to artistic problems tirelessly. His influence is evident in Sanasardo's way of using earlier dances as raw material for later work. Like Weighardt he avoided the connotation of commodification implicit in a commitment to "finished work." Other elements of Sanasardo's training were the design and construction of sets under the tutelage of Paul Sills for Tin Can Theater, "Tonight at 8:30, and Playwrights Theater Club, the forerunner of The Second City. Sanasardo also studied ballet in Chicago under Frances Ellis and learned the Wigman technique under Beatrice Stongstoff.

Sanasardo studied with and became the dance partner of the German modern dancer Erika Thimey in Washington, D.C., during the early fifties.[35] Thimey, who lived in the back of her Dance Studio, showed him that a dancer could live and work in relative solitude, very much like a painter. She encouraged him to dance professionally and introduced him to her teacher, Hanya Holm. But once in New York Sanasardo gravitated toward Graham's school. The greatest influence on his

She [Sokolow] was an encouragement for what I was already interested in — more than an influence. I understood Anna immediately; she was a real Socialist. I was part of a Trotsky group at the University of Chicago and a conscientious objector.

—Paul Sanasardo

Paul Sanasardo and Erika Thimey in her *Remorse.*

work, however, proved to be that of Anna Sokolow, perhaps the most important of the left-wing modern dancers of the thirties. Sanasardo danced for Sokolow from 1953 until 1956 and performed in the original company production of her *Rooms.* Although he did not dance in Graham's work as Feuer did, he was influenced by Graham's style through his work with Pearl Lang between 1957 and 1965. Sanasardo remained wary, however, of the "redemptive" or "affirmative" impetus in both Graham and Lang. This wariness of what I shall call affirmative cul-

It was not just class; it was to learn what Tudor was about as an artist. We learned technique from the artistic point of view, which is also a way of life.

—Paul Sanasardo

To really be primitive is to have no knowledge of art at all . . . but we all have knowledge and therefore are influenced. We shouldn't be afraid of influences.

—Paul Sanasardo

What they [ballet dancers] do is only something for the imagination to increase. If you have a beautiful arabesque, what's beautiful about it? That it doesn't stop, but something more happens, and that's in the mind of the public.

—Donya Feuer

ture, drawing on the language of Herbert Marcuse, is more than just a taste for the unhappy end. It pertains to an underlying social awareness of the history of bodies.[36]

An influence that Sanasardo and Feuer shared with equal enthusiasm was that of ballet choreographer Antony Tudor, with whom they studied assiduously at the old Metropolitan Opera House from 1957 until it closed in 1963. Tudor was their mentor. Among other things, he set an example for the relationship of teaching to choreography. "Everyone that danced for us," remarks Sanasardo, "took class with us. Today, this is unusual." Tudor was also a constructive critic of their work and introduced them to Bausch, who was dancing in the Metropolitan Opera Ballet at that time.[37]

Rather than break with their predecessors, Sanasardo and Feuer still treasure them: Sokolow remained an inspiration for Sanasardo, Graham and Chilkovsky continued to inspire Feuer, and Tudor shaped the work of both. These influences were not to be shed in the process of self-discovery, but to be remembered.[38] At the close of the Tudor era Sanasardo and Feuer continued their ballet training with the internationally known prima ballerina Mia Slavenska.[39] They also encouraged their company members to take her class. Sara Rudner remembers that other modern dancers then studying with Slavenska included Yvonne Rainer, Judith Dunn, and Deborah Hay.[40] But it was highly unusual if not unheard of at that time for a modern dance choreographer and teacher to extol the virtues of any ballet training. Sanasardo called it the period of "underground ballet." Still, a number of modern dancers studied with ballet teachers who met their needs rather than those of ballet students.

Sanasardo and Feuer made allusions to traditional ballet in their choreography. For example, in *Excursion for Miracles*, Margaret Black danced on pointe in a section on the death of Romanticism. Building on this interest in ballet training and technique, and the appreciation of its traditions of theatricalism—the effect, for example, that an arabesque *penché* might have immediately following a grounded contraction—Sanasardo later actually became somewhat of a classicist with respect to the technique he required of his dancers. In *Step by Step with Hayden* (1977) he uses music in a Balanchinian way. This eclecticism, when it appears in his work, lends it an intriguingly heterogeneous quality that defies categorization.[41] Two of Feuer's films—*The Dancer* (1994) and *The Working of Utopia* (2000)—are paeans to classical training. But, more than classical training per se, the films celebrate the process of making dancers and dances: "to create something out of nothing, a 'no' place into a 'some' place."[42] In *The Dancer,* Feuer explores the relationship of classical ballet to a young girl's desire for art. *The Working of Utopia* deploys montage as a choreographic instrument to blur perceptions of class, rehearsal, and performance, suggesting qualities of Feuer's choreography—indeterminateness, multiplicity, and intensity. Sanasardo's classicism was paradoxically linked to the class consciousness that influenced him in Sokolow's work. *O baile dos mendigos* (*Beggar's Ballroom*), created for the Gulbenkian Ballet in 1974, was his most pointedly class-conscious ballet. It was created as a reaction to his perception of class barriers in Lisbon, where he had been invited to create a new ballet.

Classical aesthetics thus constituted for Feuer and Sanasardo a common terrain of attraction, as is confirmed by the fact that classes at Studio for Dance always began at the ballet barre. Ballet positions and balances that trained the legs were combined with modern exercises that trained the back. Work in the center began on the floor, as in a modern dance class, after which the class stood up and did an adagio or slow movement. Then sequences were developed that moved across the floor.

Literary Influences

Literary modernism, especially in the works of Rainer Maria Rilke, Gertrude Stein, and Virginia Woolf, was no less influential on their choreography. Feuer and Sanasardo also shared a cult-like admiration for Isak Dinesen. Rilke's focus on childhood suffused Feuer's *Dust for Sparrows,* the collaborative *In View of God,* and her later *Ej blot til lyst* (*Not Just as Amusement*) (1985). This last work drew textually on the fourth of the *Duino Elegies* and visually on the sculpture of Rodin, who was also a strong influence on Rilke. (Both

> The integration of ballet and modern dance made very strong and versatile dancers.
>
> —Regina Axelrod

The influence of Rodin: Sanasardo and Elin Siegal in Sanasardo's *Because of Love* (1958).

Rodin has been an enormous influence in my life. You find that some people who have been here before we have, have understood, or can give us some way to think, or permission, or a kind of greeting, open doors, try, give.

—Donya Feuer

choreographers felt Rodin's impact.) Sanasardo's dance drama *Doctor Faustus Lights the Lights* (1957) was adapted from Gertrude Stein's play of the same name. Feuer's *A Serious Dance for Three Fools* (1957) was adapted from Virginia Woolf's *The Waves*. Vaslav Nijinsky's *Diaries* influenced *Excursion for Miracles* (1961) and inspired Feuer's two-part film on Nijinsky, *Ett liv* (*A Life*) and *Requiem för en dansare* (*Requiem for a Dancer*) (1978), on which she collaborated with Nijinsky's wife, Romola, and Leonide Massine.[43]

Diane Germaine, Janet Panetta, Joan Lombardi, and Michelle Rebeaud in Sanasardo's *Consort for Dancers* (1975). Photo: Lois Greenfield.

Feuer was at the time of writing working on a Shakespeare project for young children that was inspired by fifty-four letters that Ted Hughes wrote to her about Shakespeare and that form the basis for his book *Shakespeare and the Goddess of Complete Being* (1992). Sanasardo returned to choreography and text in 1975 with *Consort for Dancers,* his acclaimed setting of Anne Sexton's poetry.

Literary influences have manifested in their work as text as well as theme. Their use of text in combination with dance in the early period prefigure Feuer's subsequent work with movement and choreography in theater and opera.[44] This includes not only her dual practice of choreography and direction but also her contribution to Ingmar Bergman's work in the many genres with which she has been associated as choreographer and as performer since Lars Forsell's *Show* (based on the life of Lenny Bruce) in 1971.[45]

Ways of Moving

Sanasardo's presence in space was sculptural; his arm and leg spans were impressive. By perfecting his ballet technique, he strove to improve the centering of his body, but his artistic impulse often carried him toward tension and disequilibrium. "My energy is somewhat

facing: Studio portrait of Sanasardo (circa 1962). Photo: Zachary Freyman.

above: Sanasardo in rehearsal.

trapped," he has said. "Things bounce back onto me all the time."[46] His impetus to devour space counteracted the classical tendency to exist harmoniously within it: As Jacques Baril wrote, "His arms seem to want to take possession of space, while the semicircular movement of his leg draws that space toward the center of his body."[47] His pliant rib cage lent sculptural definition to subtle torso shifts, as if within this powerful frame were a more diminutive, fragile body. His torso conveyed a zone of vulnerability contrasting with both classical control and expressionism.[48] "If Paul were not very serious," Feuer has said, "we wouldn't have worked together. We met in this kind of seriousness. But he was very extroverted." Bausch remembers, "He made it possible for us to meet. Luckily, Paul was direct. He made many things possible." Despite Sanasardo's "dark" side as a performer, he was and is expansive, warm, talkative, and exquisitely humorous offstage. His humor, however, emerged fully onstage only in *Pictures in Our House*, a work about his Italian roots.

Feuer was a more private person than Sanasardo— reflective, internal, and less accessible. Small and compact, she radiated high energy and singular absorption. Blackstone remembers that when she first met her, Feuer struck her as "a young, intent, dark-eyed woman whose body seemed as taut and impassioned as a forest animal."[49] Art Bauman says that Feuer was "the first one to cut her hair real short and slick it back. . . . And she'd get on stage and she was Lilith."[50] For Ellen Marshall, Feuer "was a very fiery and intense poetic person, extremely inspiring because of her intensity." Modulating as well as creating a foil for this intensity was her fleeting quality and her sense of understatement. For example, in her solo *With Love* (1954), Feuer used the brief time of the dance to state departure as affective lingering. Rather than entering to dance, what Feuer performed was essentially an exit, which, once complete, created a powerful sense of her absence, and thus the impression of lingering implicit in the phrase "with love" when it closes a letter.

Both choreographers accentuated the work of the arms and upper

above: Studio portrait of Feuer (circa 1963). Photo: Zachary Freyman.

overleaf: Feuer in rehearsal (left). A strange complement: Sanasardo and Feuer in *Excursion for Miracles* (right).

torso, a tendency that would be carried further by Bausch. The stage personalities of Sanasardo and Feuer were, however, dynamically inverted. He projected himself at the audience, while she drew the audience toward her. He was tall and dramatic, she small and intimate. "We were two very separate people," said Feuer. "We were a strange complement."

The Dancer's Contribution

Style itself is a form of group dynamics.
—David Shapiro, "Art as Collaboration"[51]

Throughout their careers both Feuer and Sanasardo have stressed the dancer's contribution, even at the expense of a signature style that many choreographers prize as a trademark. Sanasardo asserted in a 1977 interview: "I don't know what my *thing* is. I am a person in relation to other people."[52] Feuer remarked in a 1999 interview, "I am very dependent on the people I work with, and I am careful about choosing them. I want to know that they are irreplaceable. There is so much we can replace, but I think people we cannot, and artists we cannot."[53] Both recall Tudor having said, "I don't want dancers. I want people who dance." Bausch has expressed similar convictions about the interpreters of her work: "I pick my dancers as people. I don't pick them for nice bodies. . . . I look for the person, . . . the personality."[54] While teaching and in more informal moments, they observed their dancers, which gave them the ability to craft movement that revealed the dancer's personality. In my conversations with Sanasardo he has rarely taken credit for this way of making choreography, referring to it instead as a kind of theft.[55] "Down with choreographers," he has said, "up with good dancers. Give me a handful of very interesting dancers and I can make something. This is partly why I taught all my dancers; while I was training people I was learning about them."

Sanasardo is fond of referring to "characters without a play" when describing the process of creating a dance: "You have people, and eventually a ballet comes." This corresponds to Feuer's concept of utopia (from her film *The Working of Utopia*): "making of nowhere a somewhere." In *Six Characters in Search of an Author* (1921) Pirandello established a precedent for "the confusion of frames," which Michael Kirby saw as the basis of the "nonmatrixed" theater of the sixties. (Frames are the theatrical landmarks that ground character and action in the matrix of conventional theatrical representation.)[56]

We were choosing each other, not pulling people out of nowhere. We didn't just make ballets. We found people. We trained people to convey what we could see. Theater is a place of existence. It had a form which is in some way the form of intuition itself.

—Donya Feuer

Dance is one of the most compromising arts in the world, because you are building it on people. It is fragments of the enormous thing we go through living.

—Paul Sanasardo

Sanasardo and Feuer confused the frames of adulthood and childhood, of modern dance and popular culture. But the confusion of performer and character is a more subtle if decisive aspect of their frame confusion. Kirby notes that "role playing becomes primary in determining matrix."[57] I believe that story is more crucial, because it does not follow that nonmatrixed work abandons roles entirely. Roles were sometimes played with self-aware superciliousness, fostering a critical distancing from, or an intentional distortion of, the idea of portrayal. Thus roles were both rejected and maintained. They were maintained inasmuch as they were part of everyday life. When person and role become difficult to untangle, narrative becomes highly ambiguous.[58]

It is sometimes assumed that nonmatrixed choreographic practices were by necessity antitheatrical or paratheatrical. However, before everyday behavior onstage became synonymous with neutrality, there was a distinction between the ordinary person and the ordinary movement: the ordinary actions of an unordinary person or the unordinary actions of an ordinary person became real possibilities. Nonmatrixed performance was not only about the leveling of differences (the democratic ethos emphasized in Sally Banes's account of the period), but about intensities of *states of experience*. The collaborative work of Sanasardo and Feuer was tangential to their experience, without a transcendental vector. They did not retreat from life into art or take refuge in aestheticism, nor did they intentionally confuse art with life. Their dances were neither expressionistic nor conceptual, neither psychological nor formalistic. For them, frame confusion is the possibility for singular or noncoded experience.[59]

Words for Conversation

PAUL: I don't think anybody at that time ever mentioned our names separately. My friends said "Paul and Donya;" Donya's friends said "Donya and Paul." We were always referred to together as if we were married. We were kind of inseparable. We both had separate sexual lives. So there was a third element. We never slept together, yet we couldn't have been closer. I never had a relationship as close as I had with Donya, as intricate, as complex.

DONYA: In making the studio, suddenly, with the two of us together, I understood that we were free. Before we met each other we each

I remember thinking that at least in dance nothing gets between you and the art. You *are* the art—you are the medium. When you are painting, when you draw, you have paint, canvas, brushes between you and your vision. In dance, you embody it. Of course, if you don't, then you only have yourself to look at.

—Ellen Marshall

had our own development. But being together made it possible to be what I would like to call "safe." The world really could *be* just what this was, and nothing else. I think it was *that* that was so beautiful about Studio for Dance, that it was filled with this kind of energy, and belief, and way to work, and dedication. And it was also a kind of liquidity where courage was not a question: everything was possible, nothing was *im*possible. You could talk about beautiful things, you could talk about brutal things; all of it belonged to something bigger than that. And that dimension, it's something I have had always, one way or another.

MARK FRANKO: It's like something that's enabled to happen between people, rather than *by* someone.

DONYA: Exactly.

JUDY BLACKSTONE: Something that explodes inwardly that's so rich.

DONYA: And it makes you secure. It's a confirmation. And I think it's possible that this is what you felt when you [Judy] met me, and when we began to work. Suddenly, perhaps, I confirmed things in you which you had felt and had no way to . . . there was nothing in the reality of your life. . . . I mean, if you're gifted, if you have this possibility, there is no other alternative. Because just having the gift leads to something which is exploration.

JUDY: It is a level of depth. It's like an air that you usually can't get to breathe—a level of fineness or depth.

DONYA: It's an expression, and a language for that depth. Even in a time of crisis or desperation, or madness, it still belongs, is part of something; it belongs to something, which is.

WILLA KAHN: There is a feeling when the curtain goes up. First of all the physical sensation of a whoosh of air coming in, that feeling of "oh my god," of being totally exposed. I have had two cesarean sections, and I was terrified; I didn't know what they were going to do. All of a sudden, while you are lying there, your little hospital gown comes up in your face. It's like the curtain going up. They actually put it on a frame, like a proscenium arch, and they clip it. To me it was a very similar feeling of tremendous vulnerability.

MARK: I do remember a sense of loss I had to give in to when the curtain went up that was both magical and appalling.

JUDY: In *Cut Flowers* they pushed me out over that abyss on a swing hanging upside down.

PAUL: Thank god for all your training. You were able to handle it.

WILLA: It was hypersensitive awareness in a dangerous situation linked to a physical sensation of the cold air coming in.

February 1, 1964: What Was Seen

February 1, 1964: my surprise on entering the theater. An exposed space, the stage literally denuded. No wings either, only fire walls of striated, burned, discolored brick. Hunter Playhouse in New York City as a sinister cavern. The stage lights, pipes and all, are dropped practically to the ground, where they cast small, intense specks of light. Some stools and chairs scattered about at random. Behind the rows of low-hanging lights, a higher pipe, to which a mass of painted canvas is attached, looking shredded and bloodied. A devastated curtain.

Audience find seats while women move about onstage at unexpected intervals. As if in a backstage area or insignificant place, a dancer with a pair of high-heeled shoes in one hand sits on a chair to slip them on. Another unselfconsciously dons a kimono, talks to someone invisible, checks a corner of the stage, disappears. City sounds filter dully through the theater. One dancer at the left downstage corner pauses to stretch in a somewhat stylized reach, lifting both arms to her right side and up to her shoulder level and above. A personal moment, but theatrically pronounced. Boat whistles. The women who come and go on the stage pull their kimonos tightly around them, hugging themselves at the waist. Is it cold? Is it morning? Weirdly slowed-down recording of a

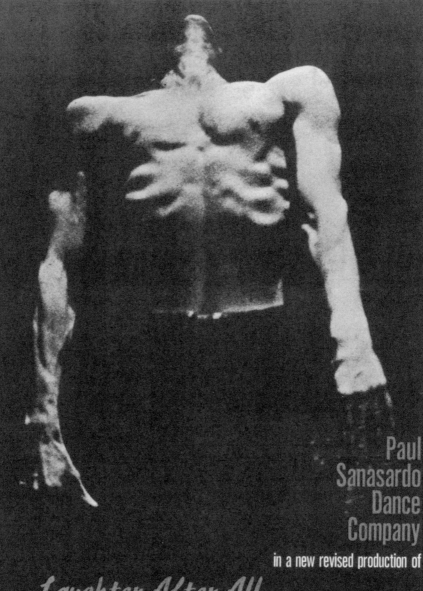

Paul
Sanasardo
Dance
Company

in a new revised production of

Laughter After All

with Diane Germaine, Manuel Alum, Willa Kahn, Loretta Abbott, Judith Blackstone, Barbara Dolgin, Sally Bowden, Regina Axelrod, Rena Raskin, Deborah Lee, Arthur Bauman, Judith Canner, Tony Catanzaro, Dennis Wayne

| MUSIC | SOUND ENGINEER | SET AND COSTUMES | LIGHTING |
| EDGAR VARESE | JAN SYRJALA | ROBERT NATKIN | NICOLA CERNOVICH |

HUNTER PLAYHOUSE
68th STREET BETWEEN PARK & LEXINGTON

Saturday, February 1, 1964 • 8:40 P.M.
ALL SEATS RESERVED PRICES $3.50, $3.00, AND $2.50

TELEPHONE: REgent 7-7482   BOX OFFICE SALE FEB. 1, ONLY
MAIL ORDERS TO STUDIO FOR DANCE.   51 WEST 19th STREET   NEW YORK 11, N.Y.
OR TELEPHONE WATKINS 4-4960, CHELSEA 3-2786   CHECKS PAYABLE TO STUDIO FOR DANCE

facing: Sanasardo's torso on the poster of *Laughter after All* (1964). The image is from Anna Sokolow's *Rooms*.

above: The Five Women in High Heels just before the initial curtain drop (L to R: Loretta Abbott, Sally Bowden, Barbara Dolgin, Rena Raskin, Regina Axelrod) in *Laughter after All* (1964). Photo: Keith Brian Staulcup.

woman's laughter. Between each drawn-out peel, a gasp for air. Hardly recognizable sounds. Moaning? The lights dim over this continuous, distorted laughter.

Act 1: "Fall on Your Face." The front curtain falls, removing from view the Women in High Heels. Almost immediately, however, it lifts again.[1] Fire alarms sound. The dropped light apparatus gradually rises from the ground, and the lights spread their pinpoints into broadening pools and then disappear aloft. The violated curtain unfurls at back and flattens into a canvas splashed with erratic shapes. Like other works by Robert Natkin from the late fifties and early sixties, this backdrop has a theatrical quality in its vertical dimensions, sensuous color, and hieroglyphic-like notations.[2] Curtain wings fly down from above. These changes, occurring in overlapping moments, are stealthy and noiseless. The stage as a place of display magically comes into being before our eyes.

The Five Women in High Heels, like the theater itself, are now "dressed": flimsy kimonos and boa stoles over the leotards and ankle-length tights of modern dance. The kimonos are lined with feathers at the neck; one has feathers along the lower hem. The women stand in line on a low platform before the unfurled backdrop. Will this now become a performance?

The Women face the audience and "vamp." Gunshots ring out, as in a shooting gallery. With each shot, one of them is "hit": a leg flies up; a back is turned; a robe falls from a shoulder. The robes eventually drop to the floor. Their boa stoles are now tied; they thread each one through a leg and around a hip. Typewriters tapping and cash registers ringing. The Women file off the platform and march toward the audience, stamp their legs in a wide "second position," and balance there while rotating their heads back and crying out "me-ow."

Coming forward, they remove their shoes and point them down toward the floor, a shoe in each hand, as they stamp in a straddled balance on their toes, dropping their heads backward and screaming. Much of the choreography for this part of the work has the Women in lines or "walk arounds." These patterns, however, are never uniform. Invariably, the Women do different things at different times.

They dance with a shoe in one hand, limping on the other high heel. They beat the pointed shoe heel rhythmically against the other palm. They meow, hiss, and scream to the sounds of jackhammers, which suggest a scene of industrial labor. The sounds they make, although violent, are done with a physical assurance, an ease with mediating voice and movement. The screams are not of shock or frozen horror, they call forth something beyond sexual objectification. They are shocks that liberate the body from its use as a mere commodity. To scream with abandon for no apparent reason requires a physiological openness, which is felt as openness onto a different dimension of experience. It is an unmotivated, free screaming in motion. The Women walk closer and closer to the ground, where they ultimately sit to beat the heels of their shoes into the floor.

Fire alarms. (Alarms begin and end each section of the work.) Varèse's *Octandre.* A quartet for "two men" and "two women." Their movements

The Five Women in High Heels from *Laughter after All* (1964) (L to R: Regina Axelrod, Rena Raskin, Sally Bowden, Barbara Dolgin, Loretta Abbott). Photo: Keith Brian Staulcup.

are lithe and animal-like. The men, however, serve largely as props for the women. These figures break through the claustrophobia of the work's beginning. "A Celebrity" saunters through: very young, flaming red hair, white spangled and bejeweled leotard, white net tights, white high heels, and carrying a whip. She is like the Women in High Heels, but as surplus rather than exchange value: the privileged figure of their degradation, a cultural symbol of their work as pure profit. She emits bloodcurdling screams but appears otherwise blasé and tends to drop her head straight backward and hug herself at the waist. Looking at the audience, her eyes participate in the scream's intensity but also mask that intensity by projecting it at the audience. High glamour, but

A Young Man (Manuel Alum) and a Girl (Willa Kahn) in act 1 of *Laughter after All* (1964).
Photo: Keith Brian Staulcup.

at the same time a certain built-in critique. She appears at other moments supercilious and self-satisfied.

Later, she enters holding a chain at the end of which is tethered a leaping, bare-chested male dancer ("her pet"). Each time she screams, she tugs on the chain and her pet falls from the air to the floor. Close to the floor, he hops beside her puppy-like and looks up adoringly. She smiles smugly at him and at the audience. Her performance is a demonstration of the self-conscious control from which she derives great pleasure. As they exit, others enter: a Young Man and a Girl perform an isolated duet while the quartet is still in progress. The patterns painted on their costumes resemble those on the curtain, but against a white rather than a black or red background. Like refugees from another world, these lone romantic figures move tentatively through the work, as if wrapped in the blind cocoon of their dance. They are the unalienated, alienated from alienation. But, in this sense, they are entirely unreal, or untouched by the world: innocents.

"Density 21.5" (solo flute): a solo dance for One Man, Sanasardo in a brown leotard and tights, wearing a gorilla wig with other, different wigs tied to his knees. "One" means one among many, but also "a particular man." He is not exemplary but is singular. He is "inward" (eyes almost closed) but also maniacal. A gesture of this solo is to lift one leg in toward the other, foot pressing against inner thigh, and one arm reaching above his head. He is fetal, tense, dangerous, but also delusional and creative. Sensitive and poetic, this figure exhibits a fury as well as an art: he can be brutal and unpredictable in his passion. His solo blends into a duet with One Woman, who wears a tan leotard and tights, with blond wigs tied to her knees. She runs to him; he lifts her and throws her backward over his head. He repeatedly throws her to the ground. Repeatedly, she rises and returns to him. This is a competitive, challenging, and physically dangerous relationship. There is no sensitivity, sensuality, or tactile exchange. In its mutual involvement, however, there is a residue of sexuality. He is abusive; she is passionate, energetic, and unsubmissive. The recorded laughter returns, speeded-up. The duet ends with One Woman on his shoulders. Totem-like, they depart in this shape.

Unsubmissive, she expends her energy bonding with him after every assault. Although it might have a psychological explanation, the relationship is uncanny in its physical terms. In the 1960 version of *Laughter* there were three characters: the Man, His Companion, and One Woman Alone. His Companion (Feuer) was passionate, whereas One Woman Alone (Chifra Holt) was more passive. The avatar of this trio was *Phases of Madness*. In the 1964 version, one dancer (a role created for Diane Germaine) embodied both these qualities, which increased the psychological complexity of the figure and the relationship.[3]

Act 2: "For God's Sake." The curtain rises, but the separation of house and stage is purely formal. Most of the cast (except the Celebrity) sits

Chifra Holt, Donya Feuer, and Paul Sanasardo rehearsing the trio for The Man, His Companion, and One Woman Alone in the first version of *Laughter after All* (1960). Photo: Mary Alice McAlpin.

Sanasardo and Feuer in *Laughter after All* (1960). Photo: Mary Alice McAlpin.

on chairs and stools in a wide semicircle onstage facing the audience. In its quality of waiting, the scene suggests a rehearsal. Just as the beginning of act 1 questioned the notion of a theater as a place of display, the beginning of act 2 consciously confuses performance, rehearsal, and event. Everyone knows everyone. The Women in High Heels no longer have high heels. A dancer slumped in a chair pares an apple with a knife, removing the skin in one long, spiraling strip. An element

Sanasardo explained that their desire was entirely determined by feeling, was not fetishized.

—Mark Franko

of task work within an overall dramatic context, it takes her the whole scene to complete. The others also have something in hand to eat. But primarily they watch. With a particularly malevolent expression, One Man stares at One Woman, who is standing and walking toward the audience when the curtain opens. When she appears to be leaving, One Man pounds his foot on the floor. She stops in response to the aggressiveness of his pounding but does not turn. She walks again; he pounds again: she stops. He rises and goes to her. The onlookers begin to exit. An extended duet ensues. There is something fascinating about this duet in that instead of depicting abuse, abuse emerges in dancing terms, that is, from the very movements performed. A lift, for example, becomes a throw; an intricate interlacing of bodies becomes a stranglehold. Differences between dance and violence are not dramatically demarcated in the performance.

A transitional scene: Five Women on chairs and stools (without high heels) reaching toward the light that comes in a narrow beam from one corner. They pull away and hide their faces. They reach again. They are not threatening and taunting here but are contemplative; they allow the audience a space for reflection. Here they function subtly as a chorus, the conscience of the work, redirecting its negativity. In the words of Hegel, "This is the portentous power of the negative; it is the energy of thought."[4] The couple of innocents crawl onto the stage and roll over one another. The Women watch them with nostalgia.[5] In this most peaceful scene of the work, the Women's voyeurism transforms to introspection.

The Celebrity's last scene: She is dressed in a black, sequined bodice. The Women in High Heels are now dressed as men: pants, shirts, brimmed caps, and street shoes. They appear only in profile or from the back, standing threateningly near the downstage wings and then moving slowly toward the center with a sudden broad transfer of

facing: The slap to the head in the Sanasardo-Feuer duet from act 2 of *Laughter after All* (1960). Photo: Mary Alice McAlpin.

The Celebrity (Judith Blackstone) meets the Five Women in High Heels in drag in *Laughter after All* (1964). Photo: Keith Brian Staulcup.

weight, dragging one foot behind. The Celebrity approaches them, bravely haughty. She lifts one leg and provocatively places it over the back of a chair. They push the chair out from under her leg but take a "wait and see" attitude. They surround her and she sits. They come closer; one reaches out to caress her face. She looks up, looking terrified, lonely, and abused: she receives this caress and is devastated by it. The chair is suddenly pulled out from under her. She tries to hold onto it but collapses to the floor. Total loss of composure. On her stomach, she stretches out her arms, catches the two rear legs of the chair, lifts it in the air, and pounds it down in front of her as far as her arms will allow. She then drags and twists her body up to the chair. With impotent fury and enormous theatrical strength, she lifts and pounds the chair, then crawls after it as if catching up. Her red hair flies in every direction as she makes her way offstage, writhing hysterically.

Lying on a hospital cart, a Young Man and a Girl are rolled onto the stage. Both are nearly naked in flesh-colored trunks and rubber hospital caps. He lies on his back and she is draped over him, face down. About seven people grouped around and on boxes and chairs watch this scene as though it were a show. One Man lifts the couple's limp bodies from the cart, sets them upright with their arms wide open,

below and overleaf: Sanasardo tortures the innocents (Jack Weber and Jane Degen) before onlookers as Feuer exults in *Laughter after All* (1960). Photo: Mary Alice McAlpin.

jumps madly up and down in anticipation, winds his arm up like a pitcher to the sound of a drumroll, and punches each in turn. Each blow is punctuated by a crash of symbols. One Woman hovers around One Man as an accomplice in this macabre exercise. Placed on their feet, the victims stand by themselves but remain otherwise immobile, with eyes closed, as if drugged or anesthetized. There is something clinical but also patently surrealistic about this scene. When One Man hits an arm, the other flies up. The onlookers laugh at these reflexes. At each stunt, One Man laughs maniacally but voicelessly, holding his head in his hands while hopping on one leg. Feuer rolls on her back like a monkey in fits of mirth. She leaps onto his shoulders. She is his best audience.

facing: Regina Axelrod and Sally Bowden abuse Sanasardo after his downfall in the final moments of *Laughter after All* (1964). Photo: Keith Brian Staulcup.

The woman's recorded mechanical laughter returns, this time at normal speed. After various experiments with both figures, One Man hits them both in the back, kicks them behind the knees, and hauls their collapsed bodies back onto the cart. They are then wheeled offstage. One Man and One Woman perform a short and uncharacteristically tender duet, after which she steps aside. The others leave. He throws himself repeatedly to the floor, pitching his upper body in a dive to the ground from a standing position. His audience leaves; some of the Women dig their heels into his back as they go. In the 1960 version, One Man cries alone on a chair. In 1964 we are left with a final image of One Man in a frozen posture, diving from his knees to the floor, head covered by his hands, foot pointed in the air as the others desert him.

Lyricism and Disaster: Mysteries of Vision

I think we were as much children as they were;
or they were as much adults as we were.
—Donya Feuer

Dust for Sparrows (1958)

The first young dancer to contribute decisively to the Sanasardo-Feuer creative process was ten-year-old Judith Blackstone.[1] Her performance in Feuer's *Dust for Sparrows* foreshadowed the provocative, intriguing, and haunting roles that more than one child would play in later works. This twelve-minute duet was rehearsed at Marjorie Mazia's Brooklyn studio in Sheepshead Bay, where Feuer taught children once a week, and premiered at the Henry Street Playhouse on February 22, 1958.

The piece begins with two brief solos for "The Girl as Child" (Blackstone) and "The Girl" (Feuer), danced to Anton Webern's *Six Pieces for Orchestra*. Amber and rose stage lights unify Blackstone's white slip and Feuer's long, dark orange dress of raw silk.[2] Blackstone's first two solos are composed mostly of jumping, stretching, and looking. "Get frightened and stare around," her notes read, "then let the strangeness leave." Blackstone recalls "running on stage and looking all around like a child discovering. I was not an accomplished technical dancer, and these were simple movements. But,

We worked on this choreography for what seemed like a long time. I felt like it was just the two of us in this studio. It had this intimate quality of two people interacting.
— Judith Blackstone

It was very simple, but, like the Webern music, we don't know what holds it together.
— Donya Feuer

49

Donya Feuer in *Dust for Sparrows* (1958). Photo: Mary Alice McAlpin.

Judith Blackstone's entrance in *Dust for Sparrows* (1958). Photo: Mary Alice McAlpin.

there was a sense of mystery to them." The child and the adult follow independent paths but ultimately meet.

Feuer enters very slowly, almost invisibly. She walks in profile but also has vertical jumps that land softly with little hops, and a daring fall onto one knee. Lillian Moore has noted the contrast between Feuer's "intense and serious concentration" and Blackstone's "simple, aimless patterns."[3] But Feuer also moves dynamically, and Blackstone's concentration after her initial carefree entrance is absorbing. Moore limits her description to the opening moments of this short piece.

The turning point occurs when Blackstone approaches the edge of the stage:

> I am walking toward the audience with my eyes closed. It is a long walk, about thirty steps, and I must keep very alert, because if I walk too far, I might fall off the stage. So I carefully slide my foot forward along the ground each time before I step. I am imagining that I am outside, walking on earth and soft grass. When I have counted thirty steps, I stop and kneel down, keeping my eyes closed. Then with my right hand, I begin to rub the ground. As I rub, I slowly open my eyes.[4]

Blackstone elaborates: "It is like seeing for the first time. It is an awakening of the senses—probably a metaphor for the deepening of the senses. . . . It was an amazing thing to take that walk toward the audience." It was an arresting moment for the audience as well. "They see," notes Feuer, "the child actually struggling with the fact that she is walking with her eyes closed." The parallel yet distinct journeys of the two figures intersect here. They meet as the music moves from Webern to de Falla's lullaby, *El niño*. They dance together. As the dance ends, Feuer lifts Blackstone and carries her carefully and protectively from the stage.

Each figure's consciousness is framed by time already lived or time not yet lived: time remembered or time anticipated. Both are on simultaneous but distinct trajectories. What joins them are "things thought, felt, seen, heard, and dreamed," as the program note specifies. Things thought and dreamed frame the senses—things felt, seen, heard; or, rather, thoughts and dreams are placed on a par with sensual perception. Such "things" are what the dance shows rather than expresses.

The exclusion of things "said" points to the relation of these things to the unsayable, which is to indicate not the sublime but instead something that Rainer Maria Rilke understood: "Things are not all so comprehensible and expressible as one would mostly have us believe;

You remember your childhood, things that happen, and relationships. But you also remember growing up, the growth of maturity. I don't think that, after adolescence, you feel it [growth] that way. You feel like you're getting older, but you don't feel like you're growing up. This feeling is related to childhood. There is no manipulation; it just happens. It happens *to* you. You can remember and feel that. The experience of time is the difference between childhood and adulthood.

—Donya Feuer

facing: Donya Feuer and Judith Blackstone at the end of *Dust for Sparrows* (1958). Photo: Mary Alice McAlpin.

It was about an adult remembering
childhood as a different sensation of
experiencing time.

—Donya Feuer

most events are inexpressible, taking place in a realm which no word has entered."[5] Rilke expands on this idea, invoking the metaphor of "contour": in his *Rodin-Book*, he writes of "something which is nothing, in a rapid outline, in a contour breathlessly caught from Nature, in the contour of a contour too delicate and precious for Nature to retain."[6] This "something which is nothing"— which is unknowable and therefore unsayable—is also formulated in Rilke's *Duino Elegies:* "We don't know our feeling's shape, but only that which forms it from outside."[7] Dance shows us these contours, intercepting them in a place of existence rather than through a process of refinement. The choreographic contours are generated not so much by a dramatic encounter as by the convergence of different paths, different locations in existence. These paths are illuminated by the relationship of age to place. The stage, as Feuer realized upon seeing Noh theater in Tokyo, is and can be "a place of existence," a place where different "things" *exist* to be seen. Thus *Dust for Sparrows* delineates something akin to a field of possibility. That field of possibility is embodied by dancers. "Dancing," maintains Feuer, "is a human possibility."

In its seeming simplicity, *Dust for Sparrows* renders a complex relation (not a relationship) carried within each one: a girl *and* a child, but also a girl *as* a child. A portrait of the artist as a young girl remembered. Feuer says, "It was very much shared with Judy, as if you could say your childhood were happening at the same time you are remembering it." It is not a psychological identification. Different orders of time —aging and growth—join in the present moment. As in Noh theater, the preponderance of time as a subject of reflection renders their encounter contemplative rather than dramatic.[8] We contemplate in the dance something that it has no interest in expressing.

This evocation of childhood and adult experience itself constituted a childhood experience and a decisive event in Blackstone's life: "It was a personal story for me because it was a formative moment of my life. This is why I remember it so well. It was a positive trauma. It shattered my whole world in a wonderful way. It broke it open." *Dust for Sparrows* initiated Blackstone's artistic career. Many years later, in her film on Nijinsky, *A Life,* Feuer says, "A dancer is the most naive and innocent of artists. Exposed and speechless, they have only the eyes of their public to receive and understand them." According to Feuer the Girl as Child contains within herself the dancer's essential figure: naive

The positive trauma: Blackstone rehearsing *Dust for Sparrows* (1958). Photo: Mary Alice McAlpin.

and innocent, exposed and speechless. Inasmuch as the Girl is also a dancer, she is a child as well, and this shared activity is what joins them in one understanding. The roles separated by distinct levels of experience are joined in one "place of existence." Thus time loses its dramatic character, and the stage is the place of externality—not the reflection of one view but the space of an encounter. The effect of this duet is to remove the sense of the age differential in the quality of the encounter. One is led to see the child in the grown-up and vice versa. The temporalities of the dance are simultaneous, heterogeneous, and reflective of realities whose complexity is not embodied in any one dancer or their interior world but in the space that contains their adjacency. The function of the stage is to be the space that the Girl and the Girl as Child contemporaneously occupy. The time it takes for movements and events to occur is displaced here by the way "places" or lived locations promote different qualities of identical time.

In View of God *(1959)*

When he saw *Dust for Sparrows,* Sanasardo was deeply impressed, and he realized that there were further possibilities to be developed. Since both Feuer and Sanasardo were teaching children's classes in Manhattan, the outer boroughs, and New Jersey, they decided to invite their best students to a regular Saturday class at Studio for Dance. They rehearsed on Saturday afternoons for their first collaborative work. Sometimes the children camped out in the studio on Saturday nights so that rehearsals could continue into late Sunday afternoon. The work in preparation was *In View of God.*[9]

When one looks at the program, *In View of God* resembles a play with acts, here called "views," and characters portraying a loose family structure (parents, children, young couple). In fact, this was not the case, since the work was more imagistic than narrative. The eleven children were seen only with Feuer, herself a mysterious interloper, undefined, an outsider looking into and through the family romance. She and the children inhabit a space outside the domestic fold. In relation to

Paul and Donya made such an impression on me—I thought everyone lived like them. They lived in a studio listening to great music and surrounded by art. Later I was disappointed that the world was so awful. [The studio] was a beautiful religious place, and I felt like it was so pure. I loved it there, and I hated my house. It stuck with me from that age until now. I was in complete awe of the way they lived. They were the only two people who never compromised.

—Lynn Barr

It was almost an extension of your home, but a different home.

—Tamara Drasin

Sanasardo consults with the children during a rehearsal for *In View of God* (1959).

Sanasardo she is an elusive and fleeting interlocutor. "We live our lives," notes Rilke, "forever taking leave."[10] Here, apart from the children who accompany her, Sanasardo senses Feuer's fugitive presence.

Expanded from *Dust for Sparrows* is the sense in *In View of God* of the child and adult inhabiting distinct yet spatially overlapping domains. *In View of God* opens this situation into a larger symbolic structure involving blindness and insight. The children following Feuer are called "children in blind sight": not seeing, but trusting. At the same time, Feuer's seductiveness toward Sanasardo introduces an allegorical dimension to this imponderable connection between worldliness and mystery, the conventional and the unconventional worlds. "If God is love," reads the program note, "then life with

There was the mother, father, and the children. And then there was this entrance of death and the children coming in. And then I think it was not a question of time and not a question of roles. It was a question of stages of living, of places of living. The children were in one place; I was in another place. It showed how the father was with his son, who was later one of these children. Danny [Canner] came into us and became part of us.

— Donya Feuer

. . . and love shall make a mockery of heaven and hell . . .

CAST

DONYA FEUER	a martyr, of pride
PAUL SANASARDO	an agnostic, the thought of uncertain man
DANIEL CANNER	his son, early seeing
JUDY BLOODSTEIN	his daughter
CYNTHIA STEELE	his wife, love familiar to waiting
CHIFRA HOLT	a young woman, new to affection
JACK WEBER	a young man
ELLEN SHOOKOFF	a child, in blind sight

KATHLYN BUSHNELL   JUDY CANNER
TAMARA DRASIN   JO-ELLEN EPSTEIN
ELAINE FISCHMAN   RUTH FRANK
WILLA KAHN   NINA LEHRMAN
RANDI RUBIN   SUSAN UNDERWOOD
WENDY WOLOSOFF   as children

. . . and we swore to it because as we were only

children all that was serious and solemn

beyond reason strangely attracted us . . .

FIRST VIEW . . . . DAY IN EARLY APRIL

Intermission

SECOND VIEW . . . . TOWARD NIGHT IN NOVEMBER

Intermission

MAN'S VIEW . . . . WINTER MORNING

The program of *In View of God.*

death is his only love affair." Sorell remarks that the children "were on stage as observers and participants in a world of unrelatedness and precariously initiated gestures and movements of the adult world."[11] What adults can discover in the mute or wordless understanding of children—or in themselves as children—is something truer than what or who they presently are. The children's role as participant-observers —unwitting imitators of a precarious model—in a world of adults would be further underlined three years later in *Pictures in Our House*.

As a performance, *In View of God* does not invite linear description. It sets forth, in Sorell's words, "images that had color, poetry and inner

Paul Sanasardo and Cynthia Steele as An Agnostic and His Wife in the opening moments of *In View of God* (1959). Photo: Mary Alice McAlpin.

The only thing I would worry about was whether the children would retain the aura of the mood. We would set up a certain aura, and they would respect that aura. Well, they kept it forever; they could sustain a scene forever. There was something knowing about these children; they were extremely mature and provocative.
—Paul Sanasardo

They brought in Maggie Black very early to teach us ballet with the adults. We had ballet class, modern class, and milk and cookies. But I learned to drink coffee there.
—Judith Canner Moss

Ellen Shookoff rehearsing *In View of God* (1960). Photo: Mary Alice McAlpin.

drama."[12] Despite implying a kinship relation, the narrative does not provide a clear story for the characters to act out. Selma-Jeanne Cohen writes, "Even when the dance situations were most obscure—[the choreography] suffused the stage with a compelling intensity of mood."[13] The mood itself, rather than narrative movement per se, is the carrier of the work's drama. The drama is constructed from the interlocking yet distinct realms of family, death, and childhood. The roles of the mother (Cynthia Steele; later, Bausch), the father (Sanasardo), the children (Blackstone and Daniel Canner), and the romantic couple (Chifra Holt and Jack Weber) together make up the conventionally lyrical and, as Rilke would say, "interpreted" world. This interpreted world is also blind, unaware of the mystery of Feuer and the eleven children, who appear disinherited denizens of a separated if contiguous space.[14] Quite

Stage rehearsal shot of Feuer's entrance with the Children "in blind sight" from *In View of God* (1959). On the right, Sister and Brother (Blackstone and Canner), who communicate with the other children in games of hide-and-seek. Photo: Mary Alice McAlpin.

original here is the staging of a world of nonbeing or extratemporality that is inhabited by children. But in terms of their daily lives, this "other" world was also the world of Studio for Dance.

In *Dust for Sparrows* Feuer had staged contemporaneously lived time as tangential "space" inhabited by people of different ages. When she said that nature does not age, she also meant that time does not age. Place is constituted of inhabited time and so becomes a place of existence. One might say that the event of the meeting between the Girl and the Girl as Child in *Dust for Sparrows* is purely spatial in that it enables an encounter outside the characters' respective temporalities to occur. This is essentially antinarrative and unpsychological. Because it falls outside cause-and-effect temporality, the encounter can be considered an *event*. *In View of God* expands tangential space between heterogeneous realms to the visible and the invisible, the conventional and the unconventional, the lyrical and the disastrous. The hints of drama suggested in the playbill (for example, Feuer's role as Death in

IN VIEW OF GOD
PRODUCED BY
STUDIO FOR DANCE
CONCEIVED AND CHOREOGRAPHED BY
SANASARDO — FEUER
WITH

PAUL SANASARDO — DONYA FEUER
CYNTHIA STEELE

CHIFRA HOLT   **JACK WEBER**   **AND DANCE COMPANY**

SATURDAY EVENING MAY 2, 1959 AT 8:30 P.M. PRESENTED BY THE DANCE CENTER OF THE YM-YWHA, KAUFMANN CONCERT HALL
LEXINGTON AVENUE AT 92nd STREET. ALL TICKETS $2.00. FOR RESERVATIONS TELEPHONE ATWATER 9-2400 OR WRITE EDUCATIONAL
DEPARTMENT, YM-YWHA, 1395 LEXINGTON AVENUE, NEW YORK 28, N. Y. PLEASE MAKE ALL CHECKS PAYABLE TO THE YM-YWHA.
LIGHTING BY NICOLA CERNOVICH
NO LATECOMERS WILL BE ADMITTED TILL THE END OF ACT ONE

facing: The poster for the first performance of *In View of God* (1959).

above: Judith Blackstone and Daniel Canner as the Daughter and Son in *In View of God* (1959).
Photo: Mary Alice McAlpin.

the second version) underline this structural relationship between the visible and the invisible, being and
nonbeing.

The poster graphic suggests a symbiosis of two op-
posing states. The rootedness of the head and arms is
necessary to their upward expansion. But the rounded
base turns out to be a skull. In the same way that the underlying bone supports and gives contour to the body's
flesh, so death contributes to life by adding contour.
This "communication" between life and death gener-
ates the work's morbidity because it insists on the presence of the excluded. And the children are primarily witnesses. Cohen
recalls, "All this seems to have been visualized through the eyes of children." With directness and simplicity, the children witness the mor-

> There was always a feeling of
> imminent disaster. Not screaming
> and yelling, but something that you
> couldn't stop. But also it was full
> of a lyricism and was beautiful.
> People were striving toward these
> things and moving on this journey.
> —Donya Feuer

"The whole thing is in Judy's eyes." — Pina Bausch. Judith Blackstone rehearsing *In View of God* (1959).
Photo: Mary Alice McAlpin.

bidity of lyrical relationships and the lyricism of morbid relationships. They are not presented as innocent or pure, but it is their naked relation to things that results in their knowing without sophistication. "Oh hours of children," writes Rilke, "hours when behind the figures there was more / than the mere past, and when what lay before us / was not the future."[15] The function of lyricism in *In View of God* was to elude or forestall disaster, while the awareness of disaster's inevitability generated a supplementary lyricism as a nonfuture. This incorporation of disaster and lyricism immobilizes dramatic movement while lending a dramatic momentum. The children are intermediaries between these domains, and they move, as Rilke said, "within the gap left between world and toy."[16] *In View of God* not only expands and transforms the encounter of *Dust for Sparrows* but opens a third space of transitivity between the positions of encounter, what Rilke calls "a spot which . . . had been established for a pure event."[17]

The event is the unsayable, that which escapes preordained meaning.[18] Games of hide-and-seek and the mysterious passing along of a locket assume an intensive quality whose excitement derives from an energetic discharge across separate dimensions. Sanasardo and Feuer choreograph and stage Rilke's "pure event."[19]

Working at Play

> "Who will show the child as it is?"[20]
> —*Rilke,* Duino Elegies

Although the children had trained hard for *In View of God,* performing in the dance was presented to them as a "serious game." This kind of game relied on a considerable amount of freshness and spontaneity on the performer's part. As with a game, the outcome remains open; unlike a game, the outcome is of consequence. "You're a dancer being a child," Sanasardo said to them, "not a child being a dancer." "The children," writes Cohen, "performed with remarkably poignant concentration."[21] Sorell recounts, "From the very beginning they set a morbid

There was nothing childish. They were like adults, only very young ones: young human beings. There was nothing cute. It was very simple.
—Pina Bausch

It was very intense. I couldn't intellectually understand life and death, crosses and skulls, passion and pain. But I could feel them. We danced with the intensity we all had, but which Paul and Donya also demanded. There was no milk, but coffee made with chicory.
—Tamara Drasin

We never talked down to them. We just did what we did and somehow they related to it. These kids were right with us, and we were doing very intellectual stuff. It wasn't children's theater.
—Paul Sanasardo

The children performing *In View of God* (1959). Photo: Mary Alice McAlpin.

mood and, as they went along, achieved some stunning images that had color, poetry, and inner drama."[22] This approach had the general effect of turning professionalism on its head because it avoided the pitfalls of a false professionalism in the child performer. Even as they were rehearsing and performing with Studio for Dance, the children were encouraged to make their own work as "early personalities." Between 1959 and 1961, the group presented dances created by the children such as Blackstone's *Afraid of the Dark* and Kahn's *Want*.

In the daily reality of Studio for Dance these children were being introduced to an artistic, bohemian world. Part of the wonderment of the whole situation was that the children discovered this adult dance world up close, in the same way that the audience of *In View of God*

Kathlyn Bushnell showing a work in progress for a "early personalities" program at Studio for Dance.
Photo: Mary Alice McAlpin.

The Children place their belongings on the ground and Feuer unfurls the sail in the final scene of *In View of God* (1959). (L to R: Ruth Frank, Tamara Drasin, Donya Feuer, Ellen Shookoff, Judith Canner Moss). Photo: Mary Alice McAlpin.

This was what I responded to most in the dancers I liked to work with: they could allow themselves to go way out of control but still have it. I mean they could sustain, hang on forever at a high level of intensity —and take you somewhere else which had nothing to do with what was out there. Donya had it, Pina, Mark. You can work with a dancer on that, but you can't teach it to them. The children had that quality, and I learned a lot from that.

—Paul Sanasardo

. . . And we swore to it because as we were only children all that was serious and solemn beyond reason strangely attracted us.

—From the playbill

discovered the "mysterious" world of childhood on the stage. In other words, for the audience to discover this mystery about childhood onstage, the children had to discover the mysteries of adulthood offstage. These were the conditions of production of the "pure event."

In the final scene of act 3 the children enter in flesh-colored undergarments with smoky gray and off-white transparent shifts over them. They carry belongings, as if they are leaving home or going to "seek their fortune." The children place their belongings on the floor and lift and pull the ends of Feuer's parachute dress, spreading it in all directions and causing it to billow like a sail. It was known as the "sailboat scene."

Adults and children "in view" of one another evoke thoughts about presence, seeing, and understanding. The title contains a double meaning: within God's gaze, but also, because of the premise of God's existence. *In View of God* stages dance itself as an art demanding its own faith and belief. Here, the complex relationship between childhood, dance, and artistic imagination are all set into motion.

The "sailboat scene" in the final moments of *In View of God* (1959).

I'll Be You and You Be Me *(1955)*

Moving backward and forward in time from 1958–1959, I shall briefly discuss other works that foreshadow or extend the preoccupations of *In View of God*. Foreshadowing *Dust for Sparrows,* the first duet choreographed by Feuer for herself and Sanasardo, *I'll Be You and You Be Me,* celebrated their newly discovered relationship in a childlike terms.[23] The poet Ellen Green read the text, which was excerpted from Ruth Krauss and Maurice Sendak's children's book of the same name.[24] This dance explored the discovery of friendship through the playful conceit of changing places by exchanging identities, and the dance may have contained a suggestion of their incipient collaboration. Recalls Feuer, "The

The seriousness of children was what the dance was about. They woke up in us the seriousness and dedication that only children can give to an art.
— Paul Sanasardo

They could hang onto it and pull it so that as she started leaving, it looked like a ship sailing off to sea.
— Paul Sanasardo

Paul Sanasardo and Donya Feuer in Feuer's *I'll Be You and You Be Me* (1955).

I'll Be You and You Be Me is something that I had to treat with enormous carefulness, because it can break. It's like an eggshell. What I like about it is it's so very friendly. She's waiting for her friend, waiting and waiting and waiting. He runs; she runs. He jumps; I jump. He calls, "Watch out lady!"; I call, "Watch out lady!" He's practically my brother. We'll take walks and hold hands. A horse dreaming of the girl that's coming to find him. It's a fantastic text.

—Donya Feuer

collaboration had excitement about it and playfulness and at the same time you knew that you were in something quite holy and sacred and not to be abused but be careful with, but you were also invited, and it was available. Nothing was '*not* possible.' One might call it inspiration and one might not."

The Krauss book is neither exclusively about childhood nor exclusively "for" children. It uses the trope of childhood to address feelings that acquire ranges of intensity from shifts in perspective. "You sit on my cold feet and I'll sit on your cold feet and you sit on my cold feet and I'll sit on your cold feet."[25] This lack of differentiation between children and adults also marks Rilke's *Stories of God* (originally titled *Of God and Other Matters/Told to Grown-ups for Children*). If the stories are for children, they nevertheless pass through grown-ups, to whom they are also addressed. The stories are staged as an exchange between grown-ups; children are never told the stories themselves. Through its naive questions about identity and its boundaries, *I'll Be You* also sketches in the name of childhood the delicacy of a partnership.

Three Dances of Death *(1956)*

The first dance that Sanasardo choreographed for himself was a triptych of solos entitled *Three Dances of Death in the Grand Manner* and subtitled *Concerned not with actual death but with the melodrama of its eminent illusion*.[26] He danced it before a three-paneled screen painted by David Lund that enabled him to withdraw for quick costume changes between sections. His disappearing behind the screen at the end of each number also foreshadowed death. The dances themselves depicted the death of three personalities: the Sentimentalist, the Hero, and the Sophisticate. The "grand manner" referred to the melodramatic but also defining qualities of sentimentality, audacity, and self-control that characterized each character's final moments. Subjectivity is crystallized as identity only in the face of nonbeing and thus, as the subtitle suggests, is an effect of death's illusion. Even though it hints at a historical progress from nineteenth-century sentimentalism to contemporary skepticism or jaded "sophistication," *Three Dances of Death* encapsulates a modern sensibility of lyricism that Michel Foucault has identified with morbidity: "The 'morbid' authorizes a subtle perception of the way in which life finds in death its most differentiated figure. . . . In death it [the 'morbid'] takes on its most particular volume . . . a singular volume defined by its absolute rarity."[27] Lyricism becomes the delineation of subjectivity at the transgression of limits, which is the threshold of imaginary nonbeing. In this first solo, we have the key to Sanasardo's reputed pessimism and his romanticism.

The "grand manner" is also an indication that the "beautiful death" is possible. Subjectivity as a secret revealed in and through the illusion of death—what Foucault calls the "lyrical kernel of man"—is central to the ominous and poetic atmosphere of *In View of God*, where things move toward death precisely to fulfill themselves. In this sense, the subject is always invisible to him or her self; real and imaginary, the sub-

It must have been a special kind of love affair. We could work very closely and deeply with each other without the responsibility any erotic relationship gives. And it wasn't less deep for that.
—Donya Feuer

We loved each other very much. The relationship was very complex. It made a very thick atmosphere between us onstage. Some people thought it was a love relationship.
—Paul Sanasardo

ject eludes the symbolic order. This is another motif of the split between character/role and the narrative, since it is the illusion of the latter's entropy that enables the former to emerge. Presence suggests nonbeing, which is what constitutes intensity's lines of flight. The very act of dancing within such a construct becomes a pivotal performance outside the symbolic order—that of the event.

There is a humorous twist to the story of *Three Dances of Death*. As Sanasardo tells it, "Death of a Sentimentalist" danced to Chopin's "Funeral March" gave a touch of hilarity. His account of this dance about death, which inspired its audience to laughter, never failed to produce laughter when retold. Hearing the story of *Three Dances of Death* makes one want to see it—to be present at this complex failure of a dance to talk "seriously" about death—which becomes in its own way, and by very reason of its "failure," a success.

The manifold relation of time and identity to the choreography of childhood and death was already implicit before the use of children as dancers. This matrix of concerns also resurfaces in later work. Feuer was to return to this fascination with the child, with the adult in the child and the child in the adult, in the film *Requiem for a Dancer*. Nijinsky (James de Bolt) enters a studio, where he has the vision of little boys in a ballet class. His relationship to dance is almost like that of a child to fever. The camera focuses in close-up on the frail legs bending at the joints, and the sound of creaking—whether of floorboards or knees—makes the act of dancing into an experience of exquisite effort and emotional tension. Dancing heightens living and points to dying. The permeable borders between life and death, being and nonbeing, are those of living and dancing. The permeable borders between living and dancing, and the mutually heightening effect of one on the other, are both the background *to* and the subject *of* these works.

It was the first time we were showing off and really having a good time, with music that was very easy to dance to.

—Donya Feuer

I remember it being a very happy period. It was very different from anything that came before or that came after.

—Willa Kahn

Pictures in Our House *(1961)*

Pictures in Our House was the last evening-length work to be made expressly for the children, casting Feuer and Sanasardo as the only adults. This work stood out in their repertory for its humor and its nostalgic qualities.

Act 1 was titled "Foreign Acquisitions." It was a turn-

Poster for the first performance of *Pictures in Our House.* The photo is of Sanasardo's mother and aunt.

What was nice was that this was really his [Paul's] (and in part his parents') childhood and there were these pictures. Contributing to all of that was wonderful because it was so personal to him, it was based on people he really knew. For me it was very simple to identify with these people, to go further with it, and to work with it. We had so much fun finding the ideas. It was very harmonious, a very warm time.

—Donya Feuer

The photographs went up to about 1930. But some were going way back to the turn of the century in Italy. I had done Sean O'Casey's *Red Roses*. I had all of his autobiographies. One is called *Pictures in the Hallway*. I read those like the bible.

—Paul Sanasardo

Pictures was an "impressionistic" work. Based on Paul's impressions of pictures of his family, it was not a detailed study but a first reaction. It was like an impression of a hand.

—Donya Feuer

of-the-century scene suggested by a photograph of Sanasardo's mother and aunt as children, dressed up for a photograph. The sounds of cuckoo clocks and music boxes are intermingled with tableaux of first-generation Italian children, wearing white lace confirmation outfits. The choreography configures them in the rhythm and spatial relations of a clock. Past time is evoked as time embodied, time stopped, and time ticking. The first scene is entitled "Still Life" and is followed by "Yours with My Love," a duet for Sanasardo and Feuer suggesting a marriage ceremony.

Act 2, "Open to the Public," comprised dramatic and humorous vaudeville vignettes. The façade of normalcy often communicated by family photographs is here affectionately stripped away to reveal idiosyncrasies. In "Sorry Sam," Sanasardo danced with three children who played at being his girlfriends. Mafioso Uncle Phil and his "molls" inspired it. "On Velvet" is about Aunt Tina imagining herself as Theda Bara.[28] Dressed as an odalisque, she fantasizes stardom by luxuriating on large, gilded pillows that the children throw to her. "Those Two," later entitled "Mama and Papa," is a scene about the argumentative relationship of Sanasardo's parents, presented as a competitive ballroom dance exhibition that degenerates into a fight. The duet also reflects on fights between Feuer and Sanasardo themselves. In the end, she pushes him to the floor and sits on his back as he crawls offstage on his hands and knees. Throughout this act, children are participant-observers, miming adult actions as well as imitating the roles they play. Unlike *In View of God*, the children unabashedly observe adults' idiosyncratic behavior.

Act 3 was titled "From the Private Collection." For Sanasardo, "It was like a finale, like you'd make a finale in a ballet." This act is a carnival dream sequence, with confetti strewn on the ground and a trapeze swinging in the air. Mama and Papa dance a duet that falls apart; the children perform a blasé circus act with hoops. The scene changes to a circus, or the aftermath of a circus,

above: "Sorry Sam" in rehearsal (L to R: Judith Canner Moss, Judith Blackstone, Willa Kahn, Paul Sanasardo). Photo: Mary Alice McAlpin.

perhaps the scene of a traveling circus leaving or just arriving. The children, dispossessed of the present at the end of *Pictures in Our House*, themselves become subjects of memory. The "pure event" itself cannot be recreated. Pictures are what the children see. Or pictures act as screen memories, images of what children *imagine* they saw. The "picture" mediates between the visible and the invisible, the remembered detail and the fantastical impression. The nostalgic attitude pervading the last act suggests *deintensification*, memory as collapse of experiential intensity. As personality becomes captured in the snapshot, it becomes the object of nostalgia and loss. *Pictures in Our House* places intensity in the *past*, as a strange amalgam of the normative and the anti-normative. At the same time, madness, which the family photograph is designed to conceal, emerges in the vignettes.

Pictures in Our House, like *In View of God*, addresses the relation of the visible to the invisible. But the mystery of *Pictures* does not depend on the unsayable as much as

We were little vamps although obviously children. But it was never vulgar; we didn't do things that were beyond the pale.
—Willa Kahn

She would bite the pillow, throw it across the stage, and then run and throw herself on it.
—Paul Sanasardo

Paul came with all this material — his life — and the only thing I could say to him was yes.
—Donya Feuer

Donya Feuer and Paul Sanasardo as Mama and Papa in *Pictures in Our House* (1961).

facing: Judith Blackstone as Aunt Tina on velvet, the role she inherited from Feuer in *Pictures in Our House* (1967). Photo: Keith Brian Staulcup.

It was kind of impressionist. The first part is very nineteenth-century, in turn-of-the-century costume. The second act was like vaudeville: Uncle Phil, Aunt Tina, Mama, and Papa. The third act was like a jaded circus. It turned into a carnival and got kind of visionary. There was nostalgia there too.
— Paul Sanasardo

A publicity shot for *Pictures in Our House.* "It's a parody of those pictures of the Russian ballet. This is our idea of a ballet company. Everyone is pretending." —Donya Feuer. Photo: Jeremiah W. Russell.

on the unveiling of the underside of human relationships revealed. Whether we think of figures from our past as idealized "picture perfect" versions of themselves or as failures and eccentrics, they are "captured" in the ambivalence of the image. The movement of choreography renders that ambivalence palpable. The image of death is captured in the conceit of the photograph as a historical artifact of the 1920s, but it also has resonance for the late fifties and early sixties in more self-reflexive terms. It is the leave taking of an era. The only way to confront this passage of time was humorously.

Pictures in Our House evokes and celebrates the fleeting present that had been the first years of Studio for Dance. Here again we find the phenomenon of double viewing that characterizes much of the Sanasardo-Feuer production: the possibility of seeing one thing indirectly, as an effect of viewing something else. It is in the crosshatching of this "visibility" that the event resides.

Words for Conversation

DONYA: On Saturdays, when I was eleven or twelve years old, I danced all day and also taught one class for Nadia [Chilkovsky]. When I came home—I was within walking distance—the apartment was empty and I was free to read Nijinsky's *Diaries.* I can see exactly how it was: I am twelve years old, and there was the sofa and the radio, and it was nice and empty, and no one is coming home for at least an hour, and I'm the only one at home. I already knew I wanted to be a dancer, and I had read in the newspaper something about Nijinsky being in England in an institution. I saw pictures in *Life* magazine. I fantasized a lot about Nijinsky. I would be lying down and reading the *Diaries,* and I would close my eyes, and I would see Nijinsky as he was in *Life* magazine. I was going to meet him. He would open the door to his cell and let me in and give me the secret of dance, open up, and let me out.

Twenty-five years after his death in 1950, I was commissioned to make a documentary film about Vaslav Nijinsky, together with his wife Romola Nijinsky and Leonide Massine. The preparations took more than a year. Some weeks before the broadcast on Norwegian television, Romola and Massine saw the film for the first time. Massine wept when I talked about Nijinsky's marriage and separation from [Sergei] Diaghilev, and Romola asked me after the film, "How did you know? How did you know?" "Because we have worked together over a year." There was nothing more I could say.

You leave the period and become circus performers. You become jaded. I was thinking of Picasso's clowns—Donya had done *A Serious Dance for Three Fools.* There was Katherine Ann Porter's *Ship of Fools.* We're all playing; we're all acting. Something has passed by and there is nothing left except confetti. It's like giving children a memory.
—Paul Sanasardo

It was like pictures in our house at 51 West 19th Street, but in another costume, another era, another position. We found something that was talking about our immediate life at the time: pictures in our house.
—Donya Feuer

DONYA: I gave Judy a little turquoise metal box to keep her makeup in.

JUDY BLACKSTONE: She told me it was a workman's box. At the beginning of *Dust for Sparrows*, you [Donya] were directly across from me, and the reason I remember it is that I was to start as the Webern music comes on. I looked across to you and you had put your head against the wing as if you were praying or something. It scared me.

DONYA: I think Judy was a part of myself, as a child.

MARK: So it was memory thing for you.

DONYA: Not only, but it began there with things that I remembered and experienced as a child. It was very much a parallel search, and it began from things remembered. When she [Judy] began to do them, then she was herself, and I was there as an adult also in her journey. And the journeys met.

JUDY: I remember that in the lift at the end you were guiding me, that I had surrendered my own agency at that point.

DONYA: The Weberns are short, highly concentrated pieces. It is very much what I'd seen in the Noh drama, this way of working at so many levels. I wasn't imitating it. Everything is a journey, finding out what is under the skin and at the back of it. Everything was intuitive. When I choreographed with you, I worked with the music a lot. But when we worked together then I made it with you. And I chose you to do it. It's very clear. And it's almost something unsayable.

JUDY: Yes, it's almost unsayable because we had an amazing time in that studio. It was shorn clean of everything else. It was pure. Of course at ten I didn't have any knowledge that I did know that. It just made sense.

DONYA: You really understood me. At times I felt that I was trying to reach or come in contact with or meet things sometimes of tremendous pain, but other times of a kind of acknowledgment of the premises. I remember thinking it was sometimes like going through a fog, and other times like meeting wind and going through wind and being blown by it. And somehow Judy was an extension of that and a part of it and also herself as a child. These were things that I remember also in the music. They were so short these pieces, so intense.

MARK: And very minimal.

DONYA: Yes, very minimal. And there was everything to understand in the music. The dance very much came from it. It's like you're getting messages all the time to keep moving to it. Even improvisation, a sort of coming into the music, of intimately learning the music.

JUDY: That was the quality of those rehearsals. That's how it felt.

DONYA: I don't think I would have made it if I hadn't met you. I don't remember looking for a child. It was really made *because* of you. We could easily speak this language. It was a very special language, but there was no problem conveying it. I knew that you knew what it was to close your eyes and go toward the edge of the stage. And it was really the edge of the stage.

JUDY: I was in some very special position. I was allowed to come after school and hang out all afternoon in Paul and Bill's loft. They would be just getting up; they would be putting away the Murphy bed. I remember that because I had never seen adults sleep so late. Paul had those wonderful art books. Bill was amazing with me. He would hold me on his lap and show me Gauguin, who was my favorite.

DONYA: You were their daughter, afternoons.

JUDY: Yes, another world. I remember how serious we were. When adults came and watched and were almost aghast at the seriousness of the children. It was very serious work. We were carrying things, and walking, with a real sense that it was profound. It was very serious.

CHIFRA HOLT: It [the children's work] was not tormented. It came across as silent, and maybe having a very important secret or mystery, but not tormented.

MARK: It was a special thing on the stage to see the children.

CHIFRA: It was. The seriousness was so unusual. I have really never seen anything like what they did with the children.

MARK: It certainly doesn't suggest Duncan's use of children.

CHIFRA: No. It's not pretty.

MARK: Not joyous and extroverted, but true to children's imagination.

CHIFRA: The beautiful part of children, really.

MARK: Why would you say beautiful?

CHIFRA: Because it's as though they have a silent partner all the time. They don't need to talk to you because they have a silent partner inside them all the time. No torment, no unhappiness, just self-contained. And that's unusual to see. Like when children play —they're very self-contained. Still, it wasn't like they were playing, because they were very serious. But it was that same feeling of total involvement. On stage, it's not that they're performing for you. No. They're doing what they do, and you happen to be observing them.

————

PAUL: At about nine years old, I did what most dancers probably do. I would go into my basement and do what I guess we'd call improvisations. I would "express" myself. These were dances of death. I loved dying. I'd jump around the basement and then there would be long periods of lying. Sometimes I would die heroically. That was partly why I called it "in the grand manner." Of course, the beautiful, holy silence at the other end of the basement was the best audience you could hope for. I created an audience that was really watching in a kind darkness. If it took me a whole hour to die, they were with me.

After I went to the [Chicago] Art Institute I began to realize that people had in some way organized these emotions and feelings that are in all of us. I saw my first ballet at fourteen years old. It was at the old Ballets Russes at the Chicago Civic Opera House that I saw [Alexandra] Danilova in *Scheherazade* and *Gaieté Parisienne,* the last pas de deux of *Swan Lake* with [Alicia] Markova, and Nina Novack in *Mute Wife*. It was a tremendous experience and a little traumatic. I was very upset because they had *organized* all the things I had been more or less doing in my basement. They had an audience, the curtain went up, the orchestra played, and they even had flowers at the end. I felt cheated. I felt like the whole world was ahead of me, like I was too late already.[29]

The three solos for the dances of death were my first choreographic efforts that I intended to perform on a stage. I was trying to remember some of the things I used to do in my basement. After many hours of improvising, I was finally able to set the movements and separate the dances into three solos, each having a specific character who would approach death in a different way.

I had a three-paneled screen as a stage prop that was designed and painted by the artist David Lund. It was a collage, which he created with his discarded paint rags, and it stood on the floor upstage to the far right. After each dance I would go behind the screen and change my costume to reemerge as a different character.

The music for the "Death of a Sophisticate" was Ravel's "Death of a Princess." I wore a pair of black dress pants and a black tailored tuxedo vest with no shirt, so my arms were bare. I modeled the character after a photograph I had of T. S. Eliot with his hair slicked neatly back. I was also inspired by a statement he had made, where he said, "I see the ending in every beginning." The movements I chose for this solo were simple, pedestrian, in keeping with the character. I remember I had some long, slow slides to the floor and I kept everything in complete control. It was a sober adagio with a dark, diabolical edge. I ended the dance stepping backward with precise steps, keeping my focus on the audience, and when I reached the screen, I stood there for a moment as the lights dimmed to a slow fade-out. Originally, I wanted to do this dance while smoking a cigarette, but I was never able to accomplish this in rehearsals so I had to give up the idea.

The "Death of a Hero" was the second dance, and it was an athletic dance with big jumps and quick, sharp movements. I danced it to a short piano piece by Franz Liszt. My costume was a red, embroidered bolero jacket with white tights. It was an exhausting, high-energy dance, and at the end I did a final leap to a big crescendo in the music, disappearing behind the screen. There was a quick blackout. I chose Chopin's "Funeral March" for the "Death of a Sentimentalist." I thought this dance should definitely have a touch of Isadora Duncan, with free, expansive arm movements and an expressive and very introspective quality. I wore a white, voluminous costume, and what I remember most about the dance were the hesitant, measured steps between the beats of the march sections, and then the swirling and running around during the reprise of the melody. I wanted this character to have the time to reminisce and have long, nostalgic farewells.

Of the three solos, the "Sentimentalist" was the most enjoyable to rehearse. There was an element of improvisation in the way I structured the dance. I left the arrangements of the movement phrases open so I could rearrange them at will. In the slow, marching sections, the steps were always hesitant, between the beat, but

I changed my direction whenever I felt the need to shift my focus. The way I danced this dance was the way I remember improvising in my basement when I was a kid in Chicago. Totally self-absorbed, performing to the most wonderful audience in the world, the imaginary audience in the holy darkness at the other end of the basement. They were kind, patient, and attentive to everything that I did.

I was not prepared for the way the audience reacted at the first performance. I was barely into the dance when I heard people laughing. I kept dancing, but I became nervous and irritated; under my costume I was dripping wet. When I finished and was leaving the stage, Paul Taylor, who was dancing on the same program and watching from the wings, said to me, "That's a really funny dance." I never danced it again.

Sequels

Sanasardo reversed the formula of *Pictures in Our House* in *Footnotes* (1970). In this memory piece, a man (Manuel Alum) reviews his childhood relationships while his playmates emerge from behind movable screens. At the end, he leaves the stage as they each disappear behind the screens. As in *Three Dances of Death,* the screens (painted by Robert Natkin) are both the place of death on the stage and a metaphor for the photographic plate that contains the secret of the playmates' reappearance and their survival in and as memory.

Feuer revisited the visible/invisible structure of *In View of God* in her *Spel för museet* (*A Play for a Museum*), first performed in 1965 amid the ancient rune stones of the archaeological wing in Stockholm's Historiska Museet (Historical Museum). It was not about the interface of life and death but rather about a more ascetic, archaic, and fatalistic dimension just below the surface of contemporary bourgeois society, what Swedish director Alf Sjöberg, apropos of Strindberg, called "rites behind the bourgeois façade."[30]

The sensibility of childhood and the passage of time was also present in a much more somber key in Sanasardo's *The Path* (1972). In the first section, "Playground," the movements of a restless quartet take the uncertainty of relationships and create the sensation of play and games. Using conventional aesthetic cues—arabesque turns, jetés, leg extensions—the gestures and fluid encounters nevertheless evoke

Manuel Alum in Sanasardo's *Footnotes* (1970–1971), the last work Sanasardo created for Alum.

very singular and uncommon identities and relationships. The movement vocabulary is familiar, but the syntax is not. In the final section, "Ice," Sanasardo addresses the catastrophe of age as a couple stumbles through what may be a morgue filled with the corpses of the earlier dancers.

In the film *Dansaren* (*The Dancer*) (1994), Feuer returned to the child in the dancer. The camera follows a young dancer (Katia Björner)

Paul Sanasardo and Diane Germaine in *The Path* (1972). Photo: Oleaga.

through her training from ages twelve to eighteen. The intensity of dance training is conveyed by close-ups that dissect the neck, the face, or the arm, scrutinizing the micromovement of muscles and tendons. Feuer exposed the dual structure of visibility and invisibility in dancing by the film's tracking of the transformation of the labor of learning into accomplished technique. But the film also focuses on training by providing views at very close range, a perspective that is uncharacteristic in examining ballet. The negotiations between the visible and the invisible are thematized in the issue of training itself and exemplified in the film's opening montage, in which close-ups of the dancer preparing are intercut with close-ups of an artisan constructing a pointe shoe. From these scenes emerge the serene image of Björner's leg revolving weightlessly in the air. It is not a question of before and after or of something suppressed for the sake of the final product: the work of dance itself becomes an expressive object.

———

The following chapters take leave of children and childhood to look at *Excursion for Miracles* and *Laughter after All,* works that developed a critical theory of society by proposing intensity as an alternative to alienation.

Unexploded Bombs: Formal Reduction and the Libidinal Aesthetic

We were crazy, but sometimes we were hitting the nail right on the head. . . .
—Paul Sanasardo

My discussion of *Excursion for Miracles* will draw on concepts of the everyday that originate in fifties and early sixties sociology, cultural criticism, and art practices. By the early fifties, critiques of everyday life were being elaborated by a handful of alert social critics. In France, the first volume of Henri Lefebvre's *Critique of Everyday Life* appeared in 1945, and the second in 1962. Lefebvre equated everyday life with alienation and thus blurred distinctions between work and leisure. Michel de Certeau's *The Invention of the Everyday* (1980) belongs in this lineage of speculation about the potentials and pitfalls of everyday life. For de Certeau the everyday was a domain of eccentric consumption that eluded the dictates of production and distribution: far from being dominated by consumer society, people invent their own uses of things and thus creatively fashion everyday life. In 1950 David Riesman, with Nathan Glazer and Reuel Denny, proposed that a new character type, which they described as "other-directed," was beginning to supersede the "inner-directed" type in the urban middle and upper-middle classes. The socialization of the other-directed individual removes his or her individualism, a salient trait of the inner-directed type: "The most important passion left in the world is not for distinctive practices, cultures, and beliefs, but for certain achievements—the technology and organization of the West—whose immediate consequence is the dissolution of all distinctive practices, cultures, and beliefs."[1] Riesman and his coauthors proposed autonomy as the solution, that is, the ability to play the game while standing aloof from it. The criterion for autonomy was the ability to cultivate privacy in one's thinking that is both personally productive and socially engaged. The most likely sphere for the development of privacy that would foster autonomy is leisure, play, or art. Their chief examples of successful autonomy are composer Charles Ives and poet William Carlos Williams, neither of whom let his work life compromise his art as an essentially private endeavor; neither availed himself of bohemianism.[2] Riesman et al. credit Erich Fromm as an important resource for the notion of autonomy; Sanasardo was reading Fromm in the late forties and worked for him.

Riesman's historicized theory of character as adaptation to culture did not leave much room for creative resistance on the part of the individual. Some of his pessimism may have rubbed off on Sanasardo, who audited Riesman's lectures at the University of Chicago in the late forties.[3] Herbert Marcuse, a member of the Frankfurt school who was living in America, first warned in 1955 of a growing threat to individuality and autonomous personality in "the transformation of 'free' into 'organized capitalism.'"[4] "Autonomous personality" echoes Riesman's concept of autonomy, whereas the introjection of corporate norms suggests outer direction. But Marcuse proposed a choice, whereas Riesman concluded that autonomy was a utopian project. In 1956, in his best-selling book *The Organization Man,* William H. Whyte Jr. wrote, "We do not need to know how to co-operate with the Organization, but, more than ever, we need to know how to *resist* it."[5] Also in 1956 the social theorist and artist Paul Goodman faulted "the Organized System"—encroaching corporatism and consumerism—for what he called the "diminishing of force, grace, discrimination, intellect, feeling, in specific behaviors or even in . . . total behavior."[6] Goodman, however, saw plenty of room for subversion in everyday life.[7] Marcuse and Goodman emerged as particularly influential figures in the sixties. This may have been because their concepts of autonomy were more resistant than quietist. Two of Marcuse's books—*Eros and Civilization* (1955) and *One-Dimensional Man* (1964)—frame our period of study. Although Marcuse, like Riesman, did not see prosaic, everyday reality as redeemable, he did stress the "aesthetic-erotic dimen-

In the nineteenth century, society created capitalism. But today capitalism has created us.

—Paul Sanasardo

sion" of art as essential to a life worth living.[8] His attitude toward art—even if it did not always favor experimental art—links art to sensuous gratification and therefore, by necessity, to everyday existence. Beginning in the sixties, Gilles Deleuze and Michel Foucault would elaborate their theories of micropolitics and lines of flight (intensities) to find again a potential for resistance and change in everyday life.

I pull together these strands of early French poststructuralist thought, late Frankfurt school theory, and American sociology not so much to paint the intellectual background of the time as to unearth options for thinking about everyday life as these options surfaced in the works of Sanasardo and Feuer and also those of Paul Taylor. Like the social critics, although without a specifically honed social intent, these choreographers were responding to the loss of individuality in the face of growing corporatism.[9]

Let me be clear about the methodology through which social theory and choreography can be compared and contrasted. Feuer and Sanasardo were not reading Marcuse, and Marcuse was not frequenting the 92nd Street Y or the Hunter Playhouse to see modern dance. Just as social theory seems to come upon dance at the furthest extremity of its own theoretical imagination (as a figure of the transcendent), so dance seems to practice social theory without consciously learning it. Dance thus constitutes a critical practice of which it, and its audience, remained imperfectly aware. By the same token, one can only guess what direction Marcuse might have taken if he had seen *Excursion for Miracles* or *Seven New Dances*. Marcuse might have recognized the elements of sensuous practice in action that he was at pains to theorize and might have changed the face of sixties dance criticism and social theory alike.

My claim is that early uses of pedestrian movement in modern dance of the late fifties and early sixties were acts of resistance to the onslaught of "organization." They resisted what Marcuse was by the mid-sixties to identify as social disease, calling it totalizing "one-dimensional" thought. He coined the phrase "one dimensionality" in 1964 to designate "the closed operational universe of advanced industrial civilization."[10] He saw the salient danger of instrumental rationality as the individual's willing "introjection" of technological reality (a tendency he also characterized as "mimesis"), by which he meant the introjection of corporatist behaviors—a latter-day fascistization—that prepares the ground for consensual "social control and domination."[11] The individual's unthinking incorporation of these controls threatened to destabilize the last outposts of individual identity by colonizing private space and strangulating free will.

Poetics and Politics of Ordinary Movement

An analysis of Paul Taylor's *Seven New Dances* (1957) will serve not only to elucidate that work but also to highlight the subject and approach of Sanasardo and Feuer's *Excursion for Miracles* (1961). Taylor and Feuer first met at the Juilliard School, where they were both enrolled in 1952. Feuer was with Taylor on Martha Graham's Asian tour in 1955, and, shortly after returning to the United States, she was in the original cast of *Seven New Dances*. She, Sanasardo, and Taylor shared concerts between 1954 and 1957 under the aegis of Dance Associates. (In 1961 Pina Bausch would also dance for Taylor.) Despite the enormous divergence in these artists' subsequent development, *Seven New Dances* and *Excursion for Miracles* confront similar issues of the everyday, autonomy and ordinary movement, from different if not altogether unrelated standpoints. The everyday is a pivotal notion in art, dance, and performance of the period: as artists began to work with everyday materials, the question arose as to whether everyday life was an already colonized or a still disalienating realm. That is, could the everyday be a way to freedom and "madness," or was it already too compromised by organization?[12]

As Paul Taylor's description of the movement found in everyday life implies, the urban landscape is a sine qua non for the development of experimental modern dance into a practice that resists the dominant culture by staging ordinary movement. The necessary conditions for the production and reception of such resistance reside in the complexity and density of the urban locale—in this case, New York City. Sanasardo and Feuer ask whether resistant everyday practices are not also to be found at the most extravagantly "playful" junctures, including but not limited to popular culture—but also whether resistance is not also compromised at these explosively iconic and critically ambivalent sites. The sites at which resistant practices operate are outside any coherent order for Sanasardo and Feuer, so they develop the idea of a city within the city, which is located "outside" itself in that this "hidden" city is miraculous. *Excursion for Miracles* designates a practice of journeys to that "outside" through a travel undertaken from within it.

Artistic life is secreted away within everyday life, embedded deeply within the everyday so as almost to escape perception. In this sense, what is hidden within is also "outside."

Epic Immobility

On October 20, 1957, Taylor's *Seven New Dances* was performed at the 92nd Street Y. The five dancers wore street clothes in all but one section. This concert received a review by Louis Horst in *Dance Observer* that was completely blank.[13] With that empty space, Horst indicated that he felt Taylor had overstepped his bounds and delivered the equivalent of choreographic blankness, to which the appropriate—if exasperated—response could only be blank paper: no ink for no movement.[14] Taylor's use of stillness troubled another reviewer as well.

Anita Dencks and Paul Taylor in "Duet," a section from Taylor's *Seven New Dances* (1957).
Courtesy of the Paul Taylor Dance Archives.

Paul Taylor in "Epic," from *Seven New Dances* (1957). Photo © Robert Rauschenberg, licensed by VAGA, New York, New York. Courtesy of the Paul Taylor Dance Archives.

Doris Hering interpreted it as a "withdrawal —an excursion into non-dance," understood as a search for "the still point."[15] Stillness, indeed, was to become the discursive icon of this concert.[16]

Sustained stillness, however, was actually a feature of only one section of *Seven New Dances*, the one titled "Duet." Anita Dencks, seated on the floor, and Taylor, standing next to her, both dressed in business attire, worked at remaining motionless. Yet the stillness seems to have moved about. In a 1987 review of Taylor's autobiography, *Private Domain*, eyewitness Lincoln Kirstein confused "Duet" with another section, "Epic." In "Epic" Taylor was dressed in the same business suit and tie as in "Duet." But, rather than hold still, Taylor shifted his postures and attitudes in synchronization to the time on a telephone recording: "At the tone the time will be . . . two o'clock and ten seconds, etc."[17] Kirstein mistakenly recalls of "Epic" that Taylor held a motionless pose "for about ten, but what seemed like 20 minutes."[18] Although this sort of error is totally understandable after forty years, it shows how stillness pervades and dominates accounts of *Seven New Dances* even though stillness played only a small role.

There is a certain logic to this shift of stillness from one section of the dance to another. The silence and stillness of "Duet" would have been even more radical, one might suppose, in "Epic." Kirstein's quid pro quo serves the position that Taylor's stillness was an act of daring, and therefore almost gratuitous, choreographic reduction. It matches Horst's review, although it is a positive evaluation. But Kirstein also limits the import of *Seven New Dances* to an exquisite scandal on the order of John Cage's *4' 33"* (1952).[19] Was this influence so decisive that Taylor's stillness became the choreographic equivalent of Cage's silence?[20] This is all too pat and, I shall argue, does a disservice to Taylor's choreography. Taylor's reduction in *Seven New Dances* requires reevaluation not just with respect to the actual events that transpired onstage but also with respect to their original, historically contextualized effect. There is a gesture of resistance within Taylor's reduction, and an interest in what I shall call tactical economies of movement.

Such reevaluation necessarily entails displacing the critical fascination with stillness uneasily haunting most accounts of *Seven New Dances*. Taylor himself wrote not of a reduction to nonmovement, but of the necessity to overcome influential choreographic models, especially Graham, but also Cunningham, Sokolow, and Shearer—"favorites" to be purged.

However, there are other sources of inspiration. In search of choreographic alternatives to the venerable choreographic models, Taylor tells us in his autobiography that he wanted to "look around in the streets."

> Everywhere the city's inhabitants are on the move—objects just waiting to be found, make-dos of an untraditionalized, piebald nation, milling and walking, sitting in vehicles or on benches, tearing off after a bus, some drunk and lying flat out. Lines of restless people at banks, theaters, and rest rooms. Wads crammed into elevators or spaced artistically on subway platforms or leaning against skyscrapers. They are standing, squatting, sitting everywhere like marvelous ants or bees, and their moves and stillnesses are ABC's that if given a proper format could define dance in a new way. All is there for the taking.[21]

It is Taylor's contribution to have linked the barely nascent use of everyday movement onstage to the street, even if the street as such was not explicitly represented onstage. The above passage from *Private Domain*, a veritable manifesto of "found posture," demonstrates that the provocative stillness that disturbed critics in 1957 was less the focus of *Seven New Dances* than it was its novel framing device. Taylor noted that, when using these postures, he and the dancers found "that each posture tends to get blurred when executed consecutively, and so it's necessary to surround each with stillness. . . . [T]he stillnesses are important and are to be on a par with the moves."[22] Stillness frames not the postures per se but the moves in and out of the postures. *Seven New Dances* is not about stillness, in other words, but about the postures for which stillness acts as a foil. More important, movement occurs in the transitions between these postures.

Taylor covered his studio walls with charts of postures. Feuer remembers that tapes of everyday sounds were used in rehearsal. The choreographic procedure for the use of postures was anything but random. Once a particular posture was "lifted" from the street and put on the stage—selected, isolated, and sequentialized—it underwent a qualitative change. Syntax was the result of a "formal, objective, practically scientific format."[23] Feuer remembers that with their postures dancers were given a sequence of counts to determine the duration of each. This protocol ensured that the postures were not rendered arbitrary in appearance. The individual dancer's freedom within these constraints, although it was concealed, was an important aspect of *Seven New Dances*. One could see the dancers as both free and unfree.

Despite the formalism Taylor employed in the creation of *Seven New Dances,* the result was unexpected. The stillness framing "shapes, spacings, and timings" took on a human face. "With no dance steps for us to hide behind," Taylor remarks, "even more than is usual the sequences are revealing us as people."[24] The words "us as people" situate the dancer's performance in direct relation to an everyday reality. Despite the formal procedures that Taylor developed to stage found positions and the transitions between them, individualized traits rose to the surface. From this perspective, stillness could be considered the background against which the figure of autonomous personality stood. Again, stillness is a foil rather than a material. "Posture," says Taylor, "has become gesture."

Even as concerns the total stillness in "Duet," Taylor recounts that his interest lay not in immobility per se but in "discovering how to hold still and yet remain active in a way that looks vital."[25] This serves to focus our attention on two aspects of movement in *Seven New Dances:* the movement of the transitions and the movement within the positions (their gestural status). What did these movements within stillness or between stillnesses convey in 1957?

Marcuse describes "an inner dimension," "the private space in which man may become and remain 'himself.'"[26] "Now it is precisely this new consciousness, this 'space within,' the space for the transcending historical practice, which is being barred by a society in which subjects as well as objects constitute instrumentalities in a whole that has its raison d'être in the accomplishments of its overpowering productivity."[27]

I propose that Taylor's aesthetic reduction of movement to stillness in *Seven New Dances* created through performance this inner dimension of which Marcuse wrote. The privacy of "inner space" was also the inner space of the dancer's decision-making about how (if not when) to change position and thus also what to find and experience in the new posture. It assured the dancer a certain autonomy.

> We had to use our imagination in getting from one position to another.
>
> —Donya Feuer

Stillness in this context should be requalified as the barely visible intent to move. It is not unrelated to what Michel de Certeau called "anti-discipline," or a set of unrecorded tactics used in everyday life in advanced technological civilization.[28] De Certeau linked such tactics not just to unpredictable uses of commodities but also to itineraries through the urban space. Movement itself, providing it avoids becoming a mere instrument, can constitute a tactical area of personal initiative within stillness. It reconstitutes what Jürgen Habermas called "the intimate sphere."[29] Realized in shifts of position and in the gestural life of the position, pedestrian movement opens a domain of personal freedom and imagination, a "private domain." Sanasardo remembers that Taylor's loft could be reached only by a trap door in the floor. It was, indeed, a private and concealed space in the city.

Critics preoccupied with stillness missed something important about *Seven New Dances,* albeit something that it was hard to see. The formal procedures devised by Taylor to stage his found positions yielded personality and thus a ground for resistance to the introjection of corporate models. Taylor's reduction of the expansive freedom to move boldly through space was not antidance as much as it was a way to re-assert the values of freedom of movement *from within* the repressive ambit of one-dimensionality. The movements were apparently casual and thus intentionally distanced from the social control of the workplace. It is not protest for the rights of the masses, as in the 1930s, but rather protest on behalf of the right of the individual to inner integrity. This protest takes the form of a subversive resistance. Found positions are divorced from efficient behavior and escape accountability because they lack a means-to-an-end rationality. They are unproductive. It is not their tendency toward stillness that is noteworthy, but rather the fact that "no adequate account of them in terms of operations or behavior can be given," as Marcuse puts it.[30] To be effective they must be practically invisible. Found movements not only resist introjection, they are also so insubstantial in themselves as to be practically unnoticeable. Such invisible or barely visible movements are difficult to pinpoint and eliminate, as Marcuse notes. This is why they are so effective as resistance. They occur in transitional spaces: in hallways, at bus stops, and on subway platforms—or on stages. These very public displays of privacy thus evade surveillance. Even though Taylor, dressed in a business suit, impersonates the "organization man," whose will and individuality are eviscerated, the scene of "Epic" is the street, not the office. That is why his postures imply transit, waiting, distraction, all leading to a certain sadness. The space to explore is reduced, but the remnants of interiority, subjectivity, and hence privacy are nevertheless to be found within its confines.

Out of the Ordinary

On October 14 and 15, 1961, Feuer and Sanasardo premiered *Excursion for Miracles* at Hunter Playhouse. It was their most daring work and a performance that took up two consecutive evenings. Excess characterized *Excursion for Miracles* and was reflected in the large cast of eighteen dancers. Subtitled "An Exhibition of the Human Temperament," the first evening was labeled "Theatrical," the second "Exhibitionism." The idea of exhibition was tinged with self-conscious display, exploitation, and voyeurism. Unlike Taylor, who had sought private domains of inner space, Feuer and Sanasardo imagined the space *outside* or external to the "organized system" as an area that was overlooked, not taken seriously. *Excursion for Miracles* presented an exploded space rather than an imploded one, whose resistance was the effect of its extroversion and idiosyncrasy. It took on the character of a sprawling choreographic oddity rather than a formal experiment and explored externality as a possible terrain of the everyday in an area distanced from the organized center. In this way it was somewhat autobiographical.

"The piece just kept growing," remembers Sanasardo. "We were still choreographing at the last minute."[31] Feuer and Sanasardo frequently worked in separate studios to save time. The Sanasardo-Feuer collaboration on this work should be envisaged as a "nonobjective

It was an excursion for the miracle of a ballet that would last for two nights.
—Donya Feuer

Like a carnival space, a "dime show," it was grotesque or tragic . . . something worn out, like circuses.
—Donya Feuer

All we had to do was come to agree upon the same thing. But it didn't mean we both saw it for the same reasons. So long as we would say "fine!"—then we'd move on.
—Paul Sanasardo

corollary" to chance procedure: they did not devise techniques with which to suppress individual intent as much as procedures to multiply intent beyond recognition. Two distinct personalities were at work; they liked the same thing but for different reasons. They did not trouble to verbalize these variations. "A way of working opened up," says Feuer, "and we enjoyed playing with it." The choreographic process as well as its result evoked the exact opposite of what Marcuse called introjection: a "non-repressive order [that] is essentially an order of abundance."[32]

Sanasardo named the methodology of their process "drifting." By this he did not mean aimlessness, but rather seeking for an exterior rather than an interior.[33] With this term, we come upon the fundamental difference between Taylor's solution to the problem and Sanasardo and Feuer's solution: "drifting" seeks an exterior rather than an interior. It is precisely this movement toward the exterior that Gilles Deleuze defines as intensity.

Sanasardo and Feuer did establish certain ground rules for this "drifting." All relationships in the work were to be devoid of sentiment. "Romantic Event," for example, evokes the death of Romanticism as a pas de quatre, with three male dancers and one ballerina on pointe (Margaret Black). The men partner the ballerina with long poles but never touch her with their hands. She balances by holding onto these poles and also dives through the air at them and then hangs from them. There is a gay subtext here, and empathy for woman as solitary within the sphere of male gayness.

Other requirements were that no music composed before 1930 could be used and all costumes had to be constructed exclusively from synthetic materials. The most telling trace of these ground rules, however, is the printed program, a graph-like map of associative thinking inspired by Nijinsky's circuitous thought process as revealed in his diaries. The program's geometry of interlocking boxes undermined the audience's instinctive

We were running after our own ideas.
— Donya Feuer

After the first night was done, we had only twenty-four hours to get the second night done.
— Donya Feuer

There was a sense of drifting. We would pick up something and follow it through without worrying if it made too much sense.
— Paul Sanasardo

It could have been called *Instead of Love.*
— Donya Feuer

We were reading Nijinsky's *Diaries* and admired his repetitions and digressions — the way that, out of his madness, there emerged a pattern and a lucidity. We weren't trying to be linear. It only got confusing at the end, when it had to be performed in a certain order.
— Paul Sanasardo

CREATION	SATURDAY EVENING OCTOBER 14, 1961	INVENTION
	PART I THEATRICAL	
PROGRESS	**POWER** Chifra Holt Jack Weber and Company	SOUND TRACK
		MOSSOLOV
	MUTATION Paul Sanasardo Michelle Llauger Donya Feuer	USSACHEVSKY
	ENERGY Loretta Abbott Kai Donaldson	DODDS
	INTERPOLATIONS Jane Degan Milagro Llauger Chifra Holt Donya Feuer	RUSSELL
	DEPARTURE Entire Company	MOSSOLOV
	INTERMISSION	SOUND TRACK
EVENTS OF ANNIHI- LATION	**CONTEMPORARY EVENT** *Bill Maloney Milagro Llauger Loretta Abbott Jane Degan Diana Ramos Linda Sidon	HENRY SCHAEFFER
	ROMANTIC EVENT Margaret Black Jack Weber Bill Maloney Kai Donaldson	BADINGS
	SUBJECTIVE EVENT Donya Feuer Paul Sanasardo Michelle Llauger	HENRY USSACHEVSKY
	INTERMISSION	SOUND TRACK
CEREBRAL RECOVERY	**DISTRACTIONS** Chifra Holt Jack Weber Milagro Llauger	SCHAEFFER HENRY
	TELEPATHIC AFFAIR Paul Sanasardo Michelle Llauger Donya Feuer Brenda Dixon Ellen Marshall Diana Munzer	RUSSELL RAAJMAKERS COWELL

The program for *Excursion for Miracles* (1961).

SUNDAY EVENING OCTOBER 15, 1961		
ORGANIZATION	**PART II EXHIBITIONISM**	DESTRUCTION
		SOUND TRACK
SYNTHETICS	**DECREE OF SOLITUDE** Paul Sanasardo Donya Feuer Jane Degan Linda Sidon Bill Maloney Kai Donaldson, Brends Dixon Ellen Marshall Diana Munzer	HENRY SCHAEFFER
	ARRAIGNMENT FOR LOVE Anneliese Widman	COWELL
	APPEAL OF ENVY Donya Feuer Chifra Holt Jack Weber Anneliese Widman Paul Sanasardo	HENRY COWELL
	INTERMISSION	SOUND TRACK
PEDESTRIAN **RESOURCES**	**READY TO WEAR** Kai Donaldson Bill Maloney Milagro Llauger Loretta Abbott Diana Ramos Jane Degan Linda Sidon	UNKNOWN
	TO THE TRADE ONLY Kai Donaldson Milagro Llauger Jane Degan Linda Sidon	BADINGS
	MADE TO ORDER Diana Ramos Kai Donaldson Loretta Abbott	RUSSELL ROLDAN
	SURPLUS Paul Sanasardo Donya Feuer	HENRY
	INTERMISSION	SOUND TRACK
MANKIND **INC.**	**PRODUCTS OF FABRICATION** Entire Company	HENRY

The program is a collection.

—Donya Feuer

As with all of our works up until that time, we were building on a subtext. We presumed that in the final result the audience would get much more than meets the eye!

—Paul Sanasardo

We were interested in positions and how you could get from one position to another. Donya had worked on this a bit with Paul Taylor.

—Paul Sanasardo

It was a success in that it didn't not work. People came back, and they paid, and we got to test a lot of ideas without really thinking about it.

—Donya Feuer

search for narrative flow and contradicted the linearity of the performance's unfolding sequential order.

Feuer and Sanasardo designed the program at Bickford's Cafeteria, a few blocks from the studio, several weeks before the premiere. Given the sprawling nature of the performance, the program served as a "map" to coordinate the collaboration.[34] However, it perplexed critics and audience members. In his review Walter Terry advised, "Pay absolutely no attention to the printed program," recommending instead that one should "react to it but not try to make any sense out of it."[35] Terry found the work to be very enjoyable, like a "colorful abstract ballet." When confronted with the pedestrian elements, however,—the "bits of irrelevant humor or lonely wanderings"—Terry backtracked: *Excursion for Miracles* was "not really an abstract piece." Sanasardo says that the movement vocabulary did include "standing around, posing, posturing, stooping, [and] walking in and out." The use of such vocabulary was still new to critics in 1961. Sanasardo said that the section entitled "Departure," at the end of part 1, "was just that: a slow exit from stage for some dancers, a quick exit for others. The dancers could choose their own motor and energy." Marcia Marks reproduced the program in *Dance Magazine* with the legend: "Puzzler for innocent bystanders."[36] This comment underscored the work's exploratory qualities and portrayed the audience itself as curious flaneurs.

A Birth and a Death

> The disaster ruins everything, all the while leaving everything intact. It does not touch anyone in particular; "I" am not threatened by it, but spared, left aside. . . . [T]he disaster is separate; that which is most separate.
> —*Maurice Blanchot*, The Writing of the Disaster

A mutated birth and a catastrophic death were the ballet's framing scenes. In "Mutation," a scene from "Progress," Feuer was born into the

Feuer emerging from the barrel in "Mutation," from *Excursion for Miracles* (1961).

ballet's synthetic world. "A large white cylinder," writes Terry, "was borne onto the stage and a hand tossed bits of apparel from it and later emerged with the rest of the anatomy."[37] The barrel was sheathed in a stretchy, white synthetic fabric.

In the final scene of part 2, "Mankind, Inc.," subtitled "Products of Fabrication," the entire cast confronts the destruction of this synthetic world. An Army Air Corps parachute served as backdrop and two army-surplus bombshells were spray-painted gold and mounted on pedestals at either side of the stage. The full cast circulates around the bombs with curiosity. Gradually, the mood changes. A plastic drop of cellophane strips through which the audience views the final moments of *Excursion* acts as an invisible wall, behind which the

She appears in extremely slow motion. First a hand, then an arm, a foot, a leg, and so on. She takes the whole scene to emerge. . . . She finishes, standing on top on the edge of the barrel, which then lights up inside.

—Paul Sanasardo

Final scene, "Products of Fabrication," from *Excursion for Miracles* (1961).

As I was climbing out [of the barrel] — this is very personal — I was being born into something that was very difficult for me to understand. The feeling was — for me — that it was taking a very long time, and that this hand suddenly felt the air around me, and it was cold, and there was light when you came out.

— Donya Feuer

We all ended huddled together in the center of the stage, as though trapped in a vacuum.

— Donya Feuer

Sometimes we ran, and we went back and forth. "What's happening; what have we done?" This going forward, and weaving, and going back. It kept moving very unevenly; it wasn't four steps this way and four steps that way. It suggested a question mark left way up in the air — that was our fear, desperation, wondering, and also in some way the public's.

— Donya Feuer

cast is eventually trapped. As the frontal light gradually grows more intense, it is reflected in the cellophane; the cast disappears in the white glare that, at its apex, suggests an explosion's afterglow.

As I progress from this account of the choreographic process and the ballet's framing scenes to the reconstruction of the whole piece, my task becomes more difficult, if not impossible. It is as though a ballet has been torn up and I must paste it back together. Although aspects of *Excursion for Miracles* were later developed into other works quite familiar to me—*Metallics* and *Excursions*—the blow-by-blow description I can conjure of *Laughter after All* is impossible to summon from these fragments. Not unlike the program itself, my description is a diagrammatic mapping. The theater, the bedroom, and the garment district are the locations on this map. In thematic terms they correspond to glamour, narcissism, and exhibitionism respectively.

> We were very happy after the first night. We never felt we were putting ourselves in a precarious situation. It was really some *thing* [moves a teacup, saucer, and spoon, as if to indicate that performing the dance was equivalent to moving things around] to perform.
>
> —Donya Feuer

Glamour

Excursion for Miracles proposed three miraculous contexts for resistance to the specter of one-dimensionality. One context was the glamorous star performer's exaggerated individuality. Feuer and Sanasardo had viewed the Italian silent film *La donna nuda* (1914) at the Museum of Modern Art and were impressed by a scene in which the diva Lyda Borelli, overwhelmed at discovering her husband's infidelity, throws herself backward and crawls desperately on her knees to a couch.[38] "To see her," said Feuer, "was a kind of miracle." Borelli inspired them to think of the role of the Celebrity in *Excursion for Miracles* as a Borelli-Graham. Borelli seemed to provide the model for Graham's melodramatic style of the forties and fifties. Moreover, her roles suggested Graham's loneliness and isolation, which Richard Move has more recently developed in his portrayal of Graham in the film *Ghostlight*.

The celebrity role also provided a way to come to terms with the powerful influence of Graham differently

> It wasn't the similarity of Borelli to Graham that impressed us. It was that Borelli was the same thing as Graham. This gave us a greater freedom to be melodramatic, to do a ballet that could include a whole kind of theater. Borelli had broken the limits and had gone way over the top.
>
> —Donya Feuer

Sanasardo and Michelle Llauger in "Mutation," from *Excursion for Miracles* (1961).

than had Taylor. Rather than seek radical choreographic alternatives to Graham's choreography, a Graham surrogate was staged in the choreography. Sanasardo and Feuer dealt with the anxiety of influence by incorporating Graham as a Borelli character. Played by Michelle Llauger, the Celebrity subjugates her lackey companion (Sanasardo), who draws her around in a chair mounted on a rolling platform. Although in her service, he treats her in a brutal and abusive manner. "I danced in an obscene and almost vulgar way," says Sanasardo, "and had control of the situation." This theatrically marked cultural icon withstands the abuse that her stud inflicts on her in private. Although the victimization occurs in her private life, her vulnerability is also seen as the outcome of her public power. Here, the critique of consumerism turns on the public and private implications of the star commodity's sexual relations. Sex as the ultimate commodity creates its own "organized system," crossing public and private domains.

Sanasardo and Feuer with Michelle Llauger behind bars in "Subjective Event," from *Excursion for Miracles* (1961).

The Graham-Borelli figure appears again in "Subjective Event," a section of "Events of Annihilation," in which Feuer and Sanasardo stand on podiums like classical statues on pedestals. Llauger, observing them first from behind the bars of a cage, sallies forth "to combat idealized figures of man and woman," as Marks observes.[39] This act places the Celebrity in a deviant stance with respect to normative heterosexuality. But the couple teams up to defeat her, and ultimately drives her from the stage. Llauger does not reappear; Borelli is banished. Violence and narcissism subvert the classical ideals and heterosexual norms of the posed tableau. The loss of the charismatic individual allows for a general libidinal release without her objectification. By the beginning of part 2, all the couples lose their connection, and trios are stressed instead.

Scene 1 [of part 2], "Decree of Solitude," was the beginning of separating the characters from their previous partners and also separating everyone from each other. It started with Donya and I each dancing a solo, but almost immediately other dancers enter the stage and begin dancing their own solos. . . . The dancers choreographed their own solos, but we all were given the same amount of time. Those who entered late finished after the music.

—Paul Sanasardo

There is always a threat to a relationship. The threat of vanity was that something would take over that would destroy trust in the other. Vanity is what keeps you from being able to trust yourself.

—Dominique Petit

When I did *Excursion for Miracles* I was not going on the stage and saying I was gay, but it was there, it was showing.

—Paul Sanasardo

Narcissism

Apart from Feuer, Sanasardo, and the two guest artists (Anneliese Widman and Margaret Black), the cast was divided up into couples—although not always paired with the opposite sex. These couples evolve into threesomes, from which one person has to be eliminated, and they are eventually all separated into individuals. In the three-way relationships one person is always in control, until all the relationships are dissolved. Throughout *Excursion for Miracles* the trio destroys the ideality of the heterosexual couple. The trio was proposed as a new way to organize relationships—or rather to do away with them altogether. Trios are characterized by a libidinal conflict because one person is always displaced or left out, and this serves to underline the role of vanity in relationships.

Feuer and Sanasardo presented themselves in this work as anything but a heterosexual couple. Feuer's short hair made her look boyish, and she played Sanasardo's creation and sidekick rather than his companion. It was Sanasardo's sensual body that was on display. He used ballet positions to project vanity, although his costume suggested aspects of popular performance culture. At the end of part 1 he wore a silver lamé jockstrap and

There was a certain amount of me that liked what the ballet was: the part that was vain, self-assured. . . . I liked the way I looked, and this could improve it and increase it. I rarely used ballet "straight" onstage. Despite the ballet, I wasn't that secure in my physical appearance.

—Paul Sanasardo

facing: Sanasardo in "Telepathic Affair," from *Excursion for Miracles* (1961).

They were trying to work out costumes, and suddenly Paul got into this gold lamé unitard, and I couldn't believe it. I thought: This piece is going to look like shit. And on the stage it was fabulous; it worked and just shone. Paul had this outrageous sense of theater.

— Ellen Marshall

silver streamers hung from his arms to accentuate the full roundness of his ballet port de bras. A photo shows him standing in perfect vertical ballet position. "Part I," reported Marks, "ended in a tangle of white drapes, and waterfalls of gold tinsel fell from the arms of the dancers."[40]

Repressive Desublimation

The Borelli figure, even though coded as Graham, was not intended as parody any more than were the ballet references. One reviewer broke the code, however, and expressed veiled objections to it. Marks wrote that Feuer's gown, "which had the glisten and color of the East River on clear gray days, could have signified a timeless, nameless, ever-present element in man and nature, a sparkling surface over black depths of relentless forces. Instead, the small figure wearing it was shunted about masochistically, and the serpent symbol shone only through the sequins."[41] She seems to have perceived the Graham intertext with some frustration because she wished the figure to embody "black depths of relentless forces." The "serpent symbol" refers implicitly to Graham's *Cave of the Heart* (1946).[42] Her description of the glisten and color of Feuer's gown with reference to specific local conditions—"the East River on clear gray days"—seems more in keeping with the spirit of *Excursion for Miracles*, which contained no timeless and nameless forces. The everyday quality of the specific location in New York City held the true reference to the forces in question.

Like everyone else on the stage, Graham-Borelli was a product of the age, a manipulated character "masochistically shunted about." The image of sensuous and emotional gratification achieved by her self-indulgence proves to be illusory. *Excursion for Miracles* sought to critique emotional emptiness and at the same time, recuperate libidinous pleasure. The whole notion of the synthetic or the surface had a double edge: how much freedom and self-realization were possible in a situation whose very terms were artificial? This permitted self-indulgence begins to suggest what Marcuse called "repressive desublimation," a "spurious sense of liberation." As polymorphous perversity enters the public sphere it is no longer free. The loss of freedom is a consequence of the loss of distinctions between work and play.[43]

Excursion for Miracles prefigures some familiar issues of the sixties but also trains a skeptical, even pessimistic, eye on any sort of framework. Unlike Sally Banes, who identifies the democratic ethos as integral to the sixties avant-garde, Feuer and Sanasardo envisaged all change as coming from within a repressive desublimation.[44] This view was in keeping with the critical perspective that, I argue, was implicitly theirs. All the vanguard effects of "unfreedom," according to Marcuse, occur precisely in liberal democracy.[45]

Anneliese Widman has remarked of Sanasardo and Feuer, "They were both extremely cerebral." But this "cerebral" point of view was arrived at intuitively, independently, and, most importantly, choreographically. It did not mistake utopia for a political project.

Paradox

The self-consciousness of paradox is encapsulated in the title: *excursion*, a temporary departure of a possibly frivolous nature, in a quest for *miracles*—the two-dimensionality (in Marcuse's terms) that would forestall the one-dimensional disaster. The contrast of the ordinary with the extraordinary can be considered an attempt to preserve what Marcuse calls two-dimensional thinking. From the choreographic perspective it should actually be called three-dimensional thinking. The miracle reinterprets "the universe of common usage" as the excursion.[46] But in the fabric of common usage, the excursion is beautiful for the way it invites the unexpected.

Marcuse uses the term "mimesis" as a synonym for "incorporation": "an immediate identification of the individual with his society." Paradox resists incorporation.[47] The two-dimensional style of thought is for Sanasardo and Feuer, as for Marcuse, contradictory.[48] The figure of the miraculous happening within the everyday points to the necessity to struggle for an awareness of paradox. This can be done, as the ballet shows, through small achievements. Taken singly, excursions hardly produce the kind of earth-shattering results envisioned by Marcuse. "Today's novel feature is the flattening out of the antagonism between culture and social reality through the obliteration of the oppositional, alien, and transcendent elements in the

> The entire work was to be paradoxical.
>
> —Paul Sanasardo

> We find that there are miracles every day. We lived in a miraculous situation. We were there because we were given a task to do. We needed to justify it, say more about it, share it with the public.
>
> —Donya Feuer

higher culture by virtue of which it constituted *another dimension* of reality."[49] Instead, this "second" dimension is approached through a series of "excursions"—departures and returns—whose ambitions exceed the logical possibility of each instance and remain a figure of the miraculous. As such, the miraculous is a figure of everyday life.

Exhibitionism

The third locus of this mapping of *Excursion for Miracles* is the garment district—a working-class neighborhood in Manhattan. Ironically, pedestrian movement is considered to be beyond theatricality and in the realm of exhibitionism. The last section of part 2, "Pedestrian Resources," deploys self-conscious references to pedestrian movement, the "antidance" source very like the one that Taylor used in *Seven New Dances*. The titles— "Ready to Wear," "To the Trade Only," "Made to Order," and "Surplus"—were all taken from signs in store windows of the garment district, where Studio for Dance was located. "Surplus" was a "pedestrian" skit for Feuer and Sanasardo, who, chained to each other at the wrists, took turns blowing up a balloon with a bicycle pump. It foreshadows the anecdotal scenes that characterize some of Bausch's work in the 1990s. The balloon-inflation scene precedes the scene depicting the disaster, suggesting therefore that the duo are about to blow up the world with a bicycle pump.

In addition to the many positions that *Excursion for Miracles* took on sexual subjects, the work also implies a commentary on the network of glamorization, narcissism, and exhibitionism that result in the commodification of experience. The libidinal aesthetic is both celebrated and placed under a critical searchlight. The impurity of behaviors in *Excursion for Miracles*, regardless of their degree of conventionality or transgression, forecasts what Marcuse, in *One-Dimensional Man*, called two-dimensional thinking. Marcuse also introduced in that book the pessimistic notion of "repressive desublimation," an idea that is implicit in the critical dimension of *Excursion for Miracles*. Certain aspects of freedom

Probably the most important influence at that time was our moving downtown to 51 West 19th Street. The neighborhood was the tail end of the garment district, and the signs in the shop windows accounted for most of the titles. Everything had to be pedestrian, ordinary, mundane. We did a lot of putting clothes on and taking clothes off.

—Paul Sanasardo

We felt too privileged. There were two big windows looking at each other: those of the garment district and of Studio for Dance. We tried to change places, to say something about what would make it easier to live across from them.

—Donya Feuer

Sanasardo and Feuer in "Surplus," from *Excursion for Miracles* (1961).

may become illusory as they are integrated into other-directed culture. The only domain within which distinctions between work and play are breached without compromising freedom is dance. Sanasardo: "The dancers are the miracles." The process of producing dance and the actual doing of it are heightening activities that assure an intensification of experience. However dexterous or artful the Sanasardo-Feuer performer was, he or she also looked like someone you might see on the streets of New York: the dancers were not "done over" to fit a mold or resemble stars within a theatrical ideal. They were pedestrians who danced, unusual people contained within the folds of urban space.

What Maurice Blanchot says of the disaster might well be said of *Excursion:* "It denotes the *pas* ["not"] of the utterly passive, withdrawn from all sight, from all knowing . . . not knowledge of the disaster, but knowledge as disaster and knowledge disastrously."[50]

The two nights were a marathon for us and probably for the audience too. So many of my later works grew out of things we set in motion on those two nights. It's amazing how easily one stumbles into what will concern one for the rest of one's life.

— Paul Sanasardo

Words for Conversation

DONYA: Excursion *for* miracles means excursions *for the sake of* miracles. "Excursion" is a beautiful word.

MARK: There's an irony there because a miracle is a big thing, and an excursion is a trivial thing.

DONYA: Yes, because it's on the side of something.

MARK: Peripheral.

DONYA: It's a more beautiful word than "trip." You find something.

MARK: It's a minor trip, isn't it?

DONYA: It's small. Not a picnic. It has a discovery about it. As if suddenly in the woods there's another trail, or there's another path.

MARK: It's unpremeditated too.

DONYA: Exactly. It's spontaneous. And, you know it afterward. You don't *go* on an excursion, I think; you *know* you are on an excursion.

MARK: You *take* one, impulsively.

DONYA: It *becomes* an excursion.

MARK: You don't plan an excursion.

DONYA: You have to "ex-curge."

MARK: It's a moving away from something. An excursion is a departure, maybe also a deviation.

DONYA: In this way we were doing strange things in our imagination, in life, and about the very things we didn't understand about ourselves.

———

PAUL: I was very involved, being homosexual, with that role of being an object. I'm her [Graham-Borelli's] object, and she's more or less supposedly in control. But I'm rather rough with her. I push her around.

MARK: You are a controlling object.

PAUL: It's like an old queen supporting a young male stud. Only I had a woman here. And when you really get involved with it, you realize that she's paying the bills and he's totally dependent on her.

MARK: So the power gets expressed through the cruelty.

PAUL: He's rough with her, and he dictates to her, and puts her back on her little chair and pulls her, makes her get off. And she's very, very beautiful, and very expressive, and has a strong feeling for him. By the time this little scene ends you realize she is going to be victimized by him. This is the relationship, a rough relationship for her, but she wants it.

Sequels

Other works were subsequently developed from the material or spirit of *Excursion for Miracles*. Two of them—Feuer's *God Is Alive and in Fairly Good Health* and Sanasardo's *Excursions*—prolonged the critique and sensibility of excess. Sanasardo's *Metallics* was a direct reworking of several motifs found in *Excursion for Miracles*. The solo, originally for Anneliese Widman ("Arraignment for Love"), put the dancer in relationship to a swinging cage first used in "Subjective Event," while a pas de deux used the partnering concept of "Romantic Event."[51]

Metallics was structured as a solo followed by a duet and ended with a series of danced cross paths leading up to a meeting of the soloist and the couple. The solo is characterized by agitated but continuous fluid motion to a Henry Cowell score that proceeds inexorably and rhythmically. The solo is a tour de force requiring the dancer to project ongoing motion and impulse through a series of rhythmically scanned retards. The duet is characterized by balletic line and an elegiac mood. Much of the duet's beauty lies in its ambiguity and suggestiveness. Sanasardo cited the Japanese film *Woman in the Dunes* as his source of inspiration. The couple in this film is isolated, interdependent, passionate, but also fragile, silent, and ritualized. The pole that connects them is a line between them, a core around which they move, a form of manipulation, a sexual bond, and something that also keeps them apart. Sanasardo has remarked that ideally the solo was designed for a female performer such as Pearl Lang in her prime, and the duet for two men—he cited Robert Blankshine and Manuel Alum. It was never performed with this kind of casting, but there are several different subtexts intersecting in this work about three. Sanasardo's work during the seventies moved increasingly in the direction of an overt reflection on gay male identity.

In "The Image," a duet from *Path* (1972), two men wearing red rubber gloves perform a love duet without touching each other. Here the idea of a visually idealized partner of the same sex is combined with the power of touch interdicted and/or wounded. Sanasardo's *Abandoned Prayer* (1976), which choreographed what is likely the first male-male kiss in modern dance, had a similar theme. This ballet retold the story of Christ so that the homoerotic kiss in question had to be construed as the "kiss of Judas." This latter work reveals the conflict between desire and betrayal and recalls the trio structure found in earlier Sanasardo works.

Meanwhile, Feuer's *God Is Alive and in Fairly Good Health* (1971) took the exuberance and excess of *Excursion for Miracles* in the direction of Tanztheater before the fact. It is a benevolent look at youth culture with a varied soundscape that includes music from Renaissance to pop. *God Is Alive* is infused with the aesthetic of drifting, as testified to by Feuer's remarks (in an interview with the author) on its genesis:

"God is alive and still in good health and signing autographs in a department store" was a line from an English television program. I was told about this by chance, and it was enough to inspire me. There was a Madonna in toe shoes; then she had work boots. (It was made for Astrid Strüwer who was pregnant at the time.) She has a fur coat, a man's hat, and toe shoes, and a small suitcase. In it was the Bible. She was reading God's book because there was no way to meet him.

The ballet is filled with props such as balloons, a suitcase, handbags, coats—the detritus of consumer society. Women stand on pointe holding large coats in front of them. God rides a bicycle onstage wearing a coat and carrying a newspaper under his arm. Shedding the coat, he performs a solo in a red unitard. Classical vocabulary is interspersed with modern floor work, and everyday objects with the surrealist dimension (in the spirit of Beuys and Magritte). Both classical and modern vocabularies are framed by pedestrian gesture, both as an extension of dance occurring seamlessly at the in-point and out-point of choreography and as a scenographic

There were a lot of things we collected that we thought it was wonderful to have onstage. There was a room in the theater where everything was packed together, all the costumes from Dramaten that had been used. There was a place with racks of ties. I took it down and made a solo for Lisbeth Zachrisson where she just gets to go through these ties, and puts one on and then the other. And she remembers all these lovers. After the dance with the ties, there was a whole section where the girls put out mattresses and just listened to radios. They were each listening to music and each one had a small solo to whatever station she found. It was a cacophony and a tragic atmosphere.

—Donya Feuer

facing: Jeffrey Delson and Fatima Ekman in Feuer's *God Is Alive and in Fairly Good Health* (1971). Photo: Beata Bergström. Courtesy of Sveriges Theatermuseum.

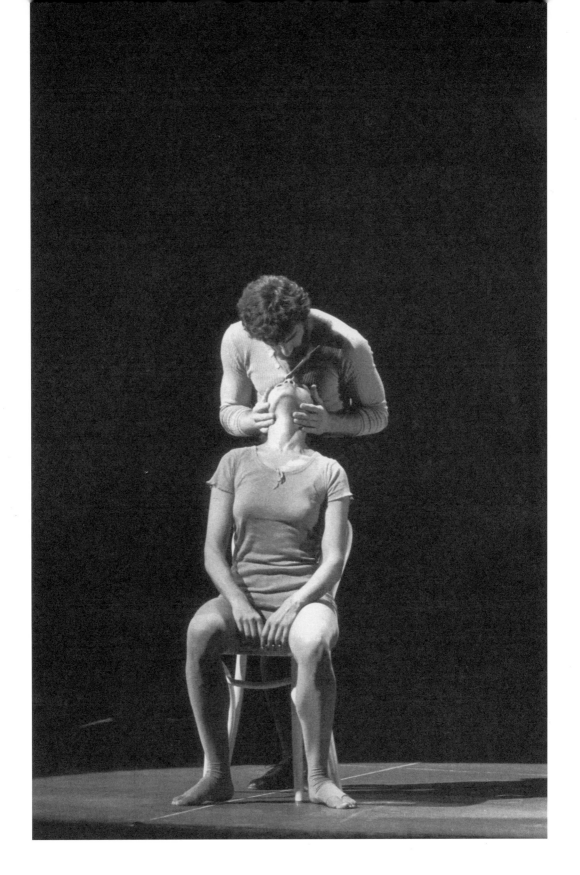

The whole theater was wide open. The balloons went up. We had taken a big Persian rug and rolled it out; there was one big sofa, some smaller chairs, and stools. It was like some strange traveling circus. Ingmar [Bergman] was doing Strindberg's *Dream Play*. One night a boy and a girl from *Dream Play* walked onto the stage in turn-of-the-century costumes. They were whispering to each other and picking up pieces of confetti and putting them in their pockets.

— Donya Feuer

frame (dancers watching other dancers). Bravura steps run fluently into, out of, and through everyday behaviors.

The solo for God, who dances while removing pieces of clothing with panache, includes turns from a kneeling position and much traveling along the floor. The floor, however, is not a place controlled by gravity but rather a space free for locomotion—an in-between space (neither elevated nor gravity-prone)—where a new level of perception occurs between the public and the private, myth and contemporary life.

The typical modern dance program of the time presented four works, the last of which was usually tongue-in-cheek. Sanasardo's decision to adapt elements of the original *Excursion for Miracles* for a shorter work called *Excursions* (1966) was in part a response to comments by critics during the sixties that his work was too serious and too ambiguous. Clive Barnes, in particular, called for humor. *Excursions* was a particularly Riesmanian work in that everyday life is seen as a contaminated realm. Most of the scenes depict leisure as false excursions from work. As Lefebvre had shown, "Leisure gives rise to an undifferentiated global activity which is difficult to distinguish from other aspects of the everyday (family strolls on Sunday, walking)."[52] In "Out Walking" Sanasardo enjoys a stroll with his head in a bucket. When he realizes that he can't release his head from the bucket, the scene turns tragic and he backs off on his knees. Buckets and stockings are the recurrent commodity leitmotivs in *Excursions*. Two women are served by two men with stockings in their mouths; a young couple flirting on a park bench find a flower in a bucket that drops from the sky. In "To the Trade Only," a remake of the penultimate scene, "Surplus," from *Excursion for Miracles,* the bicycle pump takes on phallic connotations. The couple, still chained together, confuse hobbies with sex. The care and maintenance of the bicycle is a form of leisure as technical expertise that blends imperceptibly into the technicalities of heterosexual sex through the mechanism of the bicycle pump. Working-class leisure, as it is staged here, could be at best the play of slaves, subject to strict limits. The revised skit commented on the confusion between work and leisure activity in the sense that the man is diverted from his leisure activity by the woman. Her advances turn his leisure (which is a technical activity,

Laura Dean and Mark Franko in "To the Trade Only," from *Excursions* (1966). Photo: Keith Brian Staulcup.

a kind of work) into sex, and sex into a technical activity. In this sardonic skit the pump and balloon become blatant figures for coitus interruptus, and Sanasardo opens sexual fulfillment to the specter of other "techniques." In the final scene, buckets are thrown onto the empty stage from the wings. It is unclear whether the dancers have deserted the commodity scene of the stage or thrown the buckets out of frustration, but the final image is a hostile one.

I would say that *Excursion for Miracles* and *God Is Alive* invent the kind of choreography that witnesses a moment in historical time as a set of simultaneous events—that is, events without the need of narrative sequence, without cause-and-effect "logic." Bausch's *1980* is similar in spirit and imagery. One could say that all these works take a snapshot of states of experience. *Laughter after All* develops this universe into a world that is more sustained in terms of character and more pointed toward a dialectic between madness and freedom.

Five Theses and a Coda on *Laughter after All*

The laughter was from a recording of a penny arcade.
We had a whole record of different kinds of laughter, and
we used the band called "mechanical" laughter. There was
a mechanical figure in a booth that would laugh and
pick up a card and drop it. And that was your fortune.
—Paul Sanasardo

February 1, 1964: my surprise on entering the theater . . . .

In this chapter I add analysis to the account in chapter 2 of a 1964 performance of *Laughter after All,* originally choreographed by Sanasardo and Feuer in 1960.[1] The performance was memorable because of its mediated character. "Mediation" is a term that literary critic Georg Lukács used to oppose abstraction's *immediacy*.[2] Being blind to the net of social relations isolates us in an abstract immediacy with regard to things that appear and events that happen. To perceive things or events as abstract or "immediate" is to accept their inevitability, to be seduced by the vivid presence of their "nowness." While immediate, they are also abstract because they remain disconnected from interpretation: unmediated or "im-mediate."[3] That which is immediate is unrelated to us and thus promotes reification: the becoming a thing or commodity of experience. A synonym of "reification" is "mechanization." The immediacy and factual quality of appearances paradoxically dehumanizes our relation to them.[4]

There is a productive contradiction in the idea that immediacy is

STUDIO FOR DANCE PRESENTS

THE FIRST PERFORMANCE OF

LAUGHTER AFTER ALL

AN UNSPOKEN DRAMA REVEALING THE CRUELTY AND MADNESS OF ONE MAN AND HIS COMPANION

CONCEIVED AND CHOREOGRAPHED BY SANASARDO-FEUER

WITH

PAUL SANASARDO DONYA FEUER

CHIFRA HOLT JACK WEBER

JANE DEGEN BARBARA DOLGIN MILAGRO LLAUGER DIANA RAMOS PETER BERRY EDWARD SUTTON

LIGHTING BY NICOLA CERNOVICH   SET DESIGN BY ROBERT NATKIN

SATURDAY EVENING JUNE 18th, 1960 AT 8:40 P.M. AT HUNTER PLAYHOUSE, 68th STREET, BETWEEN PARK AND LEXINGTON AVENUES.
ALL TICKETS $2.50. FOR RESERVATIONS TELEPHONE CHELSEA 3-2786 — WATKINS 4-4960 OR WRITE STUDIO FOR DANCE, 51 WEST 19th
STREET NEW YORK 11, N. Y. PLEASE MAKE ALL CHECKS PAYABLE TO "STUDIO FOR DANCE".

The Celebrity (Judith Blackstone) and her pet (Tony Cantanzaro) in act 1 of *Laughter after All* (1964).
Photo: Keith Brian Staulcup.

facing: Poster for the premiere of *Laughter after All* with drawing by Robert Natkin (1960).

JUDY: Varèse said I had a very musical scream. And that's all it was. It was just a pure scream. It was as much of a scream as one could do. And so I think it was probably interesting to hear voices just do that. A full-out scream without necessarily placing it emotionally.

MARK: How did you find that for yourself?

JUDY: I had a very loud voice, and Paul asked me to scream.

Free fall and free for all.

—Donya Feuer

reifying, or that mediation, to the contrary, is enlivening. The reified laughter in *Laughter after All* evokes that contradiction. It is all hysterical abandon, until we hear the end of its breathed cycle and perceive its mechanical program of self-repetition. What at first sounded abandoned now sounds manufactured. What appeared direct is now revealed as indirect, in need of mediation. *Laughter* was among the most direct and unrelenting of dances. In this sense, it was unlike the distorted recording of laughter and like the live screaming that also played a significant role in the piece. This sketch is interpretive as much as an attempt to reconstruct the "eventing" of this contradiction: the mediation of the recorded laughter juxtaposed to the abstract immediacy of the live screaming. The lights dim for . . .

Act 1: "Fall on Your Face"

The Five Women in High Heels are suggestive of burlesque performers. Sanasardo identified the impetus for *Laughter*'s burlesque imagery in a Detroit burlesque act whose star executed Grahamesque contractions. Yet the Women are also (especially in the second act) a modern dance "chorus." We cannot ignore the lean, stylized, trained bodies of modern dancers in the early 1960s. The reference to burlesque is complex because it draws on both a sexualized spectacle that suggests modern striptease as well as the historical burlesque of the mid-nineteenth century, in which the female performer demonstrated a threatening "awarishness," a "directness of address and complicity in her own sexual objectification."[5] Five Women in High Heels embody neither the epic presence of historical modern dance nor do they quite realistically represent the transgressive evocations of burlesque theatrics. Their effect, instead, is to blur modern dance's use value with burlesque's exchange value. "The utility of a thing makes its use value," writes Marx. "Exchange value at first sight, presents itself as a quantitative relation,

facing: Five Women in High Heels "vamp" before the Natkin backdrop in *Laughter after All* (1964) (L to R: Barbara Dolgin, Rena Raskin, Loretta Abbott, Regina Axelrod, Sally Bowden). Photo: Keith Brian Staulcup.

He had this idea about the prostitute that she never got involved emotionally. Don't lose yourself in the moment — always be in control. He had a very diabolical notion of women. They were strong and manipulative; women control men. The prostitutes were not vulnerable. They were beautiful, attractive, and seductive. You could have a relationship with them because no one was going to get hurt.
— Regina Axelrod

The shoes became a prop in the dance: a weapon and an extension of your body.
— Regina Axelrod

as the proportion in which values of one sort are exchanged for those of another sort."[6] Modern dancers as burlesque performers, burlesque performers as modern dancers: a sharp distinction between these two identities is never made clear. Much like the Detroit performer, they fetishize use value (modern dance) and humanize exchange value (burlesque).

Sanasardo refers to these characters as "the whores." Their poses and gaze are aggressive and menacing. The image of vamping that is so prevalent in the choreography for Five Women in High Heels—"standing erect, chin up, hand on hip, and right foot advanced forward, patting the floor"—suggests what Robert Allen has called the "feminization of the [American] burlesque in the 1860s."[7] But this feminization is not to be confused with sexualization. What is overemphasized is their *appearance* (not what they look like, but the fact that they are there to be seen), as if to say that theater is the market, that it is "the part [of the system] which constantly *appears*."[8] The theatricality of the Women communicates in dance the fascination with commodities.[9]

American modern dance has presented itself historically as unalienated labor. No objectification (reification) of the dancer's body is thinkable because modern dance itself cannot be considered a product separable from the body that dances.[10] Unalienated, its use value can be contaminated only by imagined or thematically repressed exchange values. Movement, process, and relation do not lend themselves to fixity, abstraction, or objectification.

"Commodity fetishism" suggests the sexual fascination of commodities in comparison with sexed human bodies, but which in turn can be redeployed across the living human body of the prostitute, the human body as sexual commodity. The commodity is an object, properly speaking; the worker's body is also a commodity in that she or he sells his or her labor. The working body of the prostitute takes the human commodity one step further, dramatizing how a worker's labor is also a commodity "inseparable from his physical existence."[11] As Christine Buci-Glucksmann pointed out apropos of Walter Benjamin, the prostitute is "the allegory of the allegory of commodities."[12] So are the Five Women in High Heels.

> *They dance with one shoe in hand, limping on the other high heel....*

The prostitute in *Laughter* is not involved in a narrative premise: there is no assignation, no striptease. She is a commodity threat, whose exaggeration unleashes other thoughts or possibilities about the relation of bodies to commodities, that is, commodified sexual relations. The Women in High Heels form a modern dance chorus mediating a logic of commodity fetishism: they act out a movement between immediate abstraction and mediated concreteness, a movement toward realization. This occurs most remarkably in the historical composite of *Laughter*'s burlesque evocations. The Five Women have voices and use them, which is characteristic of historical burlesque. As Allen attests, striptease did not dominate burlesque until the mid-1920s. He calls striptease "the form [that] focused . . . on female sexual spectacle, causing the burlesque performer to lose her 'voice' and much of her transgressive power."[13] The Five Women in High Heels wield transgressive power. They have voices. Their violence consists in wrenching from its equivocal appearance as themselves the human commodity that they ostensibly evoke. There is a real contradiction in their vamping: a strength and a weakness, a power and a loss.

We worked late at night very often on 19th Street. Paul had us going across the floor in a very small studio. We had to scream at the top of our lungs. It was more of a howl; it was eerie. I was sure the police would come, but they never did.
— Regina Axelrod

As a dancer, you were very vulnerable because he asked you to do things [for which] there was no precedent. Because it was a personal relationship, you could get hurt easily. We were all vulnerable: we were not good "prostitutes."
— Regina Axelrod

First thesis: *Laughter after All* unmasks the myth of modern dance as unalienated labor. It seems to me that one of the common tasks of 1960s modern dance was not to commodify the body, but to displace its myth of use value, often by appropriating technology.[14] The task was to cease presenting movement as a fulfillment of need, as what the dancer "needed" to do in some psychological or symptomatic way. Use value's invasion of modern dance had characterized thirties activist performance but led to theatrical representations of hysteria in the forties as well. By the 1950s it had led to a habitual association of modern dance with generalized emotionalism. Sanasardo and Feuer introduced an alienated modern dance body without "avant-garde" reference to technology. Their work reinscribed emotion within a social frame, where its very uses became dislocated. They preserved emotion as a history of need: madness, cruelty, or physicality, they also displayed emotion caught in the circuitry of production and consumption. Its historicity derives from its divorce from immediacy: it is not wholly explicable in a present or as a present. This history of need montages high culture (Graham) with low (the Detroit burlesque act) at various historical conjunctures, and surrealism with realism. It is a performance of social and aesthetic contradictions.

Repeatedly he throws her to the ground; repeatedly she rises to return to him. . . .

Although sadomasochistic couples were a familiar feature of American popular entertainment, abusive relationships were not on the conscious cultural agenda of the early sixties in the way that they are now forty years or so later. One critic said that the work lacked universality, whereas today its universality might be all too clear. Yet One Woman is not directly presented as a victim. Abuse itself seems to reproduce, to regenerate their relationship. Another critic wrote, "The Man directed his passion for physical mishandling against One Woman who, flattened consistently by blows that would have made a professional boxer reel, managed to drag herself gallantly erect repeatedly."[15] The "madness and cruelty of one man and his companion" (as the work is subtitled) is not a psychological problem of their relationship. Instead, it is a complex figure encompassing both their freedom and society's rage against it.

I could push Donya hard, and she could take it. I couldn't have done it with anyone else. She was able to cope with this kind of thing. She found her own meaning in it. She never questioned me; we never talked about it. We would do things, and she'd say, "Yes, that works; this doesn't work." We never discussed the premise of it.

— Paul Sanasardo

What was important for me was to fight back.

— Donya Feuer

Second thesis: Abuse, or "cruelty and madness," becomes a means to think about productive negativity, and I think that it should be conceptualized as negativity in that it exposes false organic harmony. Indirectly negated is what Herbert Marcuse calls "affirmative culture," the autonomy of "bourgeois subjectivity" in a separate and invariably private sphere of inwardness in which there is also, ostensibly, creative freedom. This is tradition-

Paul Sanasardo and Loretta Abbott: One Man and One Woman in their violent duet from the second act of *Laughter after All* (1964). Photo: Keith Brian Staulcup.

ally the sphere of art that cannot be touched by, and cannot affect, social processes. In other words, art is a traditionally autonomous sphere to which the private soul repairs seeking recompense for an irredeemably exploited social existence. Cruelty and abuse, however, render such a closed world of emotions and subjectivity inescapably social, for they force that world into the outside, turn it into a social disturbance. The freedom of madness to enact its cruelty is also the

I was mirroring his energy and throwing it back on him, so this cruelty was not going in one direction. It went back and forth in waves. It wasn't emotional; it was very physical activity in trying to give a form to what is cruelty, what makes something cruel. Not just an object like "he's being so cruel," or "she's being beaten up." Cruelty is a terrible image: when the rain becomes ice and it pours down on you. We wanted to work with things that were not controlled and try to give a form to things that were not controlled.

—Donya Feuer

I was out to come out of the closet. It was a slap at the establishment.

—Paul Sanasardo

madness of freedom—the unending expansion of the self into uncharted areas. It is this dialectic between madness and freedom, first emerging in the trio *Phases of Madness*, that was subsequently developed in *Laughter after All*.

Negativity is an explosion of the private into the public, of the subjective into the social; it is also the march of the personal into cruelty. Negativity is critique without a utopian proposition or a democratic agenda. *Laughter after All* depicts madness *in* the social, almost *in* a relationship. One Man is encouraged by One Woman and extends the sphere of his abuse to others. For this he is, up to a point, applauded.

Affirmative culture is by definition set apart from the "material reproduction of life."[16] Marcuse defines affirmative culture as a refuge from life—a refuge in art. In this sense, art can affirm life by standing apart from its material realities. However, what *Laughter* produces is materiality of relationships as performance, that is, as modern dance. And perhaps cruelty and madness (expressed as abuse) are the only means, short of pornography, by which human relationships can be exposed in their materiality. Before it is considered as itself, cruelty introduces a functional distance from the stock conventions of sexual difference. The uncanny pliancy of One Woman points to an impossible reciprocity, a mythical hallmark of heterosexual relations. She is a match for One Man, although they are not a "match." The characters and relationships presented without parody or irony in *Laughter after All* are in themselves illusions and, therefore, critiques of affirmative culture.

Third thesis: The heterosexual relationship in *Laughter* does not stand as autonomous and natural outside history any more than production stands as an autonomous and natural given outside history for Marx. This is Marx's starting point in *Grundrisse*, where he reframes production and consumption in almost performative terms: "One appears for the other, mediated by the other."[17] Performances, too, are products, in that they are brought into being by their own dissolution, which

The Women in High Heels reappear in drag in the second act of *Laughter after All* (1964). Photo: Keith Brian Staulcup.

amounts to their consumption by onlookers. The consumption of violence is voyeurism.

> *The Celebrity approaches them, bravely haughty. She lifts one leg*
> *and provocatively places it over the back of a chair. They push*
> *the chair out from under her leg. . . .*

When the Celebrity reappears in the second act, she is accosted by a group of "men" who are easily recognizable as the Five Women in High Heels in drag. This scene of women playing both men and women touches upon the historical character of American burlesque, which, until the mid-1920s, was characterized by cross-dressing rather than striptease. Burlesque featured vocal women impersonating males without the "intention to deceive the spectator or to suppress their femininity."[18] "Horrible prettiness" was—simultaneously—the exposure of the female sexuality inherent in women playing men's roles, the possibility that this sexuality was coded as homosexual, and the added fact that the male audience might, through some unexplained process, in fact be viewing this spectacle as one of male homosexuality. The cross-dressed Women in High Heels are, in other terms, the allegory of the allegory of male homosexuality.

The Celebrity's last scene can be seen in three ways: as her tangible violation through heterosexual consumption (the "men" transform the stage into a back alley in which they encounter the Celebrity), a lesbian gang rape, and—if one extends the transgressiveness of the burlesque to male homosexual fantasy—as a scene of male homosexual panic. It is all three interchangeably because of the ambiguous readings that one can give the cross-dressed figures and because, by extension, as a figure of surplus value the Celebrity herself can be read symbolically as a male transvestite, even though she is clearly played by a young girl. In fact, the performer's very youth supports the baroque quality of this reading by indicating a daring transference. In this way, and perhaps with a more precise set of concerns than Allen will attribute to burlesque's "political paradox," *Laughter* reproduces what he calls the "irreducible complexity of the burlesque."[19] (One of the only ways to get at that complexity, in my opinion, would be to recover, or speculate on, the kind of laughter that early burlesque audiences produced.)

Let us turn now to the ballet's final scene: the abuse of the innocents.

One Man lifts the couple's limp bodies from the cart, sets them in standing positions with arms extended to the side, jumps madly up and down in anticipation, winds up like a pitcher to the sound of a drumroll, and punches them each in turn.

In a similar manner, the final scene of the work, in which the madman brutalizes the practically naked bodies of the innocent couple, also constitutes a "consumption" of the couple's earlier romantic duet. Performing for the other members of the cast, One Man inverts their first act duet by replaying it as a duet between corpses set in motion (quite literally) by the choreographer. The work ends by consuming itself from

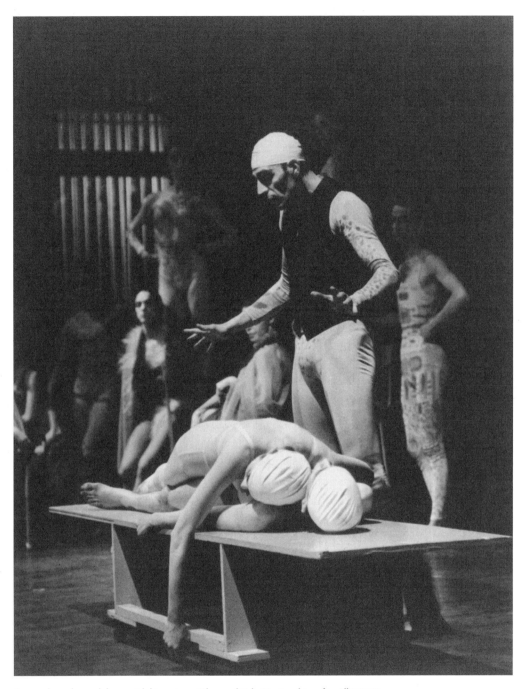

Sanasardo as the mad doctor with his patients (Alum and Kahn) in *Laughter after All* (1964).
Photo: Keith Brian Staulcup.

within (from its own creative source), reproducing itself as internal consumption of its own process, stereotypes, and theatrical scenes.

————————

Fourth thesis: The physiological action of laughter, its expulsion of air and sound via energetic ejection from the oral cavity, has a highly ambiguous negativity. Exploring this negativity is part of the strategy behind replaying the recorded "fun house" laughter at different speeds. Laughter may be the last "organic" metaphor available to the unalienated modern dance body: it contains the seed of alienation and confronts the organic with its own mechanism.

In *Laughter*'s final scenes, the work's cruelest protagonists, the Celebrity and One Man, achieve thematic totality. The link between the scream and the laugh also connects the Celebrity and One Man. The distortion of recorded laughter suggests an agony—the capture of freedom in the convulsive fit of its own rage as a practice of resistance. The live screams of the whores are figures of freedom's pass toward the irrational. The intermediate position of the Celebrity between the whores and One Man reveals a complicity between liberty and humiliation. None of these figures are representations. Rather, as in *Phases of Madness,* they are phases of a dialectic between madness and freedom, relays in states of experience. The Celebrity is the "exceptional" being who is demystified (whose surplus value is reduced to subjectivity), and One Man is the "unexceptional" being who has become a mad doctor in a chamber of horrors. The abuse perpetrated by One Man on the innocents (by the choreographer on his dancers) is, in the Celebrity's experience, the spectating abuse visited upon her by her audience. One Man's scene of madness turns the two unalienated subjects of the work—a Young Man and a Girl—into objects. Production is cruelty (performance); consumption is voyeurism (spectatorship). One Man performs for spectators who laugh but ultimately abandon him in disgust.

————————

facing: Sanasardo brutalizing the young innocents in the final moments of *Laughter after All* (1960).

Final thesis: From the 1930s through the 1960s modern dance was modernist in the way it sought organic "solutions" to the reification of modern industrial society.[20] Novel "solutions" become choreographic or pedagogically oriented "styles," some of whose signatures are Graham's contraction, Cunningham's use of chance, Rainer's pedestrian task, and so on. Each stylistic signature is an "organic" metaphor, by which I mean only that it can be theatrically embodied. The degree to which each creator can distinguish her or his self from a choreographic predecessor is the degree to which she or he can successfully deploy a new metaphor, a new aesthetic-ethical solution, a new performance of use value. Each solution implicitly proposes a new social space as style, a different training. Thus we have both the need for and the enormous difficulty of innovation.

It wasn't a question that he was getting rid of something, as if I were the object. But this kind of screaming and being hit is one of the qualities of the pain of living. This was the way things were or could be. It wasn't a question of hate or abuse. It could be fury, but it could be a kind of a scream about not just this kind of violence but that this kind of violence exists. It was grotesque. I enjoyed doing this like hell. Because people have this kind of power of destructiveness. . . . It's not a question that it was a Freudian relationship. It was a question of showing what pain really was, violence, and this very animal-like part of people.

—Donya Feuer

Laughter thwarted this modernist challenge by taking it in a distinctly negative direction. Laughter itself has been an overwhelmingly powerful metaphor for use value in Western culture. Rabelais identified it as the physical-behavioral trait that uniquely defined humanity.[21] But, *Laughter*'s laughter is reified, alienated, mechanized, and manipulated from beginning to end. It is a sign of unalienable human identity but "after all," that is, revisited ambiguously as consuming rather than producing humanity. It is this inorganic metaphor, the last embodiment that can be derived from the body, that links exchange value (the Women in High Heels) and surplus value (the Celebrity) to a critique of the "natural" (the heterosexuality of One Man and One Woman). *Laughter* was much ahead of its time in exploring not only abuse in sexual relationships but issues of gender and sexuality as well, issues that had barely penetrated the consciousness of the Left in 1960.

Coda

The generating matrix of the piece was the relationship between One Man and One Woman. This is not to say that a psychological or narrative reading would be accurate. What Feuer describes when she says that the cruelty was not "emotional" but a "very physical activity"

Sanasardo and Feuer pause during a stage rehearsal of *Laughter after All* (1960). Photo: Mary Alice McAlpin.

is intensities or intensive states. These uncontrolled actions exist on the stage as intensities.

While Feuer depicts the work as part of a process, Sanasardo views it from the perspective of his danced character: "Life was there for him to satisfy all his needs, and it was a kind of madness. He wasn't frustrated, this character, he could wheel the people out and slap them. He was having a good time until it went too far and he had violated everything. That's why I thought of madness: it's his madness he's exploring, the freedom to follow his impulses." The collaborators depict exteriority in different but complementary ways. It can be thought of as the placing of violence into real space and time, into events. As such, it cannot be measured any more than it can be controlled.[22] This violence stands as a principle of freedom against which all the other characters of this "unspoken drama" can be read: the whores, the romantic couple, the celebrity and her pet. Despite its evident abusiveness at the mimetic level, *Laughter* has an ethical dimension.

Deleuze has written about "those *states of experience* that, at a certain point, must not be translated into representation or fantasies, must not be transmitted by legal, contractual, or institutional codes, must not be exchanged or bartered away, but, on the contrary, must be seen as a dynamic flux that carries us away even further outside. This is precisely a process of intensity, of intensities."[23] He underlines the relation of intensity to externality—it "carries us away . . . outside." This might be considered escapist. But what has escaped is subjectivity. Intensity achieves its most theatrical dimension through the exploration of violence, which necessarily flirts with but ultimately evades a psychological interpretation. But the fact that it happens between people—and this relates to what has already been said about its social provenance—has no anchor in social causes, because intensities depend on aesthetic (or erotic) experience more than on interpretation. In this sense, as Lyotard notes, they cannot ground a politics.[24]

Yet we can still think of Sanasardo and Feuer in dialogue with Taylor's concerns about the melancholy freedom of internal and barely visible movement in *Seven New Dances*. Because a space for freedom of movement is no longer possible in the private or the public domain, only intensities can overcome the dichotomy of inside/outside—both of which are colonized—and discover freedom outside the self's limits. If both externally managed (corporate) and internally secreted (private) behaviors are subject to surveillance and discipline, then only intensities *exterior* to individual subjectivity resist surveillance and discipline. The quest to transgress the limits of subjectivity—phases of madness—traceable across the Sanasardo-Feuer work of the late fifties and early sixties, succeeds in the 1964 version of *Laughter after All*. This quest started with the lyric self relayed into the dispersed subjectivities of childhood; it concluded with radical alternatives to alienation.

Words for Conversation

DONYA: I think these things that we discovered, and that Paul developed even more, were sensational things, really, things from life itself. I think that's why we all reacted to it as we did. We were trying to understand the life we lived, and our dedication to it, which was also a dedication to trying to understand. Trying to understand was itself a religious act. Life is something quite serious, and to be treasured, and is easily destroyed. All this was a pursuit, in good time—I mean, before you die—for understanding something that might lead you or accompany you toward death. We both understood this, and it perhaps explains how we could work so well together. I thank God we existed; thank God the people who inspired us existed, and that we were in the right place at the right time.

On My Mother

PAUL: My mother was my beginning; for the first twelve years of my life I was her pupil. I acquired all of my best acting skills from watching her in action. She was a very theatrical woman, but her performances always took place behind locked doors. We were a large family, so situations often got out of hand. When my mother felt it was time for her to step in to straighten things out, the first thing she would say was—"Shut the windows"—and then she would release the fury of a Medea; she had the ability of a good actress. She knew how to bring her scene to a close, and when it was over, it was over.

Many years later, when I was working in New York, my mother decided to come to the city to see the premiere of *Laughter after All*. I was apprehensive about this visit; I didn't think she would enjoy this work, and I was certain she would never understand why I would choreograph a work with such cruelty and violence. After

Portrait of Paul Sanasardo. Photo: Jaacov Agor.

Portrait of Donya Feuer. Photo: Magnus Reed.

the night of the premiere, she came backstage and politely waited in my dressing room for everyone to leave, and then she said— "Paulie, shut the door!" My heart sank; I thought, "Now I'll hear it." But instead of a confused outburst, she said in a calm, clear, steady voice: "You shouldn't let people know you're like that." And then she added, "If you want to stay on the stage you should try and make people like you." She was shocked, but she wasn't even surprised. She just wanted to straighten things out and give me some of her good advice.

Several weeks later, when I had time to give some thought to what she had said, I realized she knew before I did that in many ways *Laughter* was a catharsis for me, that my true nature was exposed to the public, the outside world. She also had some commercial insight; the audience does prefer a pleasant performance. *Laughter* was not that successful with the public.

We go through life seeing ourselves in so many different mirrors, but somehow we always reflect the same presence. Those very early years of our childhood are the blueprint for everything that will happen later in life. As we get older we gain a bit more acceptance of who we really are.

Appendix A

Autobiographical Essays by Paul Sanasardo

Paul Sanasardo wrote the following three essays on the basis of our interviews. Each essay reveals an aspect of his choreographic process. "Pictures in Our House" describes the family photographs that formed the basis for that work. "The Procession" describes the roots of his religious experience relevant to *In View of God* and other works. "Riverview" gives his impressions of life in Chicago during the Great Depression, elements of which are found in *Laughter after All.*

"Pictures in Our House"

Act 2 of *Pictures in Our House,* "Open to the Public," was set in the thirties, the time of the Great Depression. It was performed in the style of vaudeville acts. There were three photographs that inspired the three different scenes, "Sorry Sam," "Aunt Tina on Velvet," and "Mama and Papa."

The photograph for "Sorry Sam" was a picture of my uncle Phil with his friend Alabama. They are dressed in pencil-stripe suits and wearing fedoras. They each have a one-hundred-dollar bill showing from the cuffs of their shirts. My uncle Phil was into gambling and bootlegging and drove around in a fabulous cream-colored convertible. When he would come to visit us, he would usually show up with a sultry woman and introduce her to us as our aunt Sherrie. Over the years we had several Aunt Sherries. He was the only man I knew who had his nails manicured, wore a diamond ring, and had money. He would pass out twenty-dollar bills to each of us, and when he would leave, my mother would collect the money and tell us not to ask any questions. In the dance I had him dancing with three women, but the women were very young girls, which gave the scene a bit of a Lolita twist.

"Aunt Tina on Velvet" was a photograph of my father's younger sister when she was still young and beautiful. She's reclining on a cluster of velvet pillows, dressed in a harem costume and looking like a Theda Bara character, although the Aunt Tina I knew was a short, plump woman, always in a house apron, cleaning her house and taking care of a flock of children. Despite the constant demands her family made on her, she had a happy disposition, and I have memories of her shuffling around her kitchen, singing one of her favorite songs, with the lyrics— "I ought to be in pictures. . . . I'm beautiful to see"—and for those of us who doubted her beauty, my mother would say, "You should have seen Aunt Tina; when she was young, all the boys wanted to marry her." The scene from Aunt Tina was entirely based on the personality of Aunt Tina in the photograph. A young girl with an excessive imagination, dreaming of sexual encounters.

Mama and Papa were of course my mother and father. In the photograph I had of them they are young, long before I was born, and they are in evening clothes. My father is wearing a tuxedo, and my mother a taffeta evening gown. They are standing close together, holding hands, looking very well-mannered and very compatible. But of course, after many years of marriage, and six children, and the difficulty of trying to keep a household together during the Depression, I remember them having heated arguments almost to the point of violence. My father protected his independence, and he had a quick temper, but my mother was a strong woman and made her demands. I never saw my father strike my mother, but he pounded his fist on the table and slammed doors.

In the scene "Mama and Papa," I had them doing a ballroom dance, but I cannot recall ever having seen my parents dancing together. For the purpose of theatricality, I brought the arguments to physical acts of violence, because it was/is a dance and everything had to be said in movement. Before the dance comes to an end, it takes a sudden turn to playfulness and indifference.

The last act, "Private Collections," was one long, nostalgic scene of memories, a finale with all the characters seen as you would see them in a dream. The setting was a carnival—a circus—we had a trapeze on-stage, hoops, and large rubber balls, and there was confetti strewn on the floor, with streamers hanging down from the pipes overhead. I was thinking of Picasso's clowns from his rose period; everything was in soft colors, and the movement was casual and easy and fun to do. It was a farewell, and now when I look back, it's strange that this was the last work that Donya and I collaborated on. Without knowing it, our working together in such a close way was coming to an end. It was not long after that Donya left for Sweden.

Pictures was not just about the characters in my family, because a lot of what we were putting on the stage was arrived at from the relation-ship that Donya and I had at the studio. For seven years we had been living and working together in the same building. The children from *In View of God* were growing up, and as compatible as we were, we were having some severe arguments.

Separations start long before they happen. And when love and re-spect are involved, it's painful, and it takes a while before the parting of the ways is realized. When Donya left to go and teach in Stockholm, it was to be for a short period of three months. But I think we both knew it was bringing to an end one of the most important periods of our lives. We had set the foundation for the work that each of us would do separately after that. Some things happen once and only once, and they are the things that are beyond comparison.

Pictures was the most autobiographical of our works. The photo-graphs were given to me by my grandmother, but they were not the rea-son, or the whole purpose, that inspired me to choreograph the work.

"Foreign Acquisitions"—the first act—was my attempt at trying to recreate the aura of the world my mother grew up in. Her parents, my grandparents, were a strong presence in my childhood, and they left a lasting impression on me. My grandmother, who I remember as a small woman with fine delicate features, had an exquisitely old-fashioned manner. She was privately religious and spent a good deal of her time devoting herself to taking care of my grandfather. He was a handsome-looking man, but he had a formidable critical nature, and I can still feel his stern, watchful eyes keeping a check on my behavior.

Together they preserved a way of life that in many ways kept time at a standstill. When I was a youth and had the desires and interests that were rushing me to the future, they in their steadfast manner managed to instill in me a deep appreciation for a past that, at that age, I had little patience for.

The place that they called home was in reality a modest apartment on the second floor of a two-story wooden building in the old section of Chicago, which today is called Old Town.

There was a steep staircase built on the outside of the house that led straight up to their front door. When you stepped over the threshold you were standing in another place in time. The rooms were embraced in silence, and the sparse furnishings were arranged in the orderly fashion of the Old World. I have no recollection of ever having heard a radio played in the apartment, and the only time you heard music was when my grandfather played his old opera recordings on the Victrola in the front parlor.

At the back of the apartment was a quaint but well-equipped kitchen, where my grandmother meticulously recreated the Sicilian meals that were served promptly and ritualistically. Behind the kitchen was a wide porch with tall windows, where my grandfather grew exotic herbs and raised a menagerie of canaries. The floors were polished and had linoleum on them, and in the bedrooms the windows were heavily curtained and the shades always half lowered. On the wall above the beds was a print of the Blessed Virgin Mary, and in my grandmother's bedroom, on a chest of drawers, was a small altar and a row of vigil candles.

Nowhere was the ticking of a clock more prominent or the sound of canaries' chirping more welcomed. And now that I'm older, I'm astonished to see how that serene way of living has found its way into my own life. How much it has become a part of who I am and how I think and work.

It was not until many years later, after my grandfather died, that my grandmother was willing to give me a small box of old, faded photographs that I took with me after a nostalgic lunch. It was a radiant afternoon late in October when I went to see her. She had been pestering the family for everyone to visit her because she had a premonition that it was her time to die, and the time would be before Christmas. When I saw her I was surprised to see how well she looked—as healthy as she did when I last saw her, which was almost ten years earlier. I asked her why she was so convinced that she would die before Christmas, and she looked out the windows into her backyard, where the wind was rustling the leaves, and she said, "You see how the leaves are falling from the tree, well, my last leaf is ready to fall; my guardian angel came to me in a dream last summer and told me the Blessed Virgin would be waiting for me around Christmastime."

Like all mysteries, which I cannot explain and have no answers for, my grandmother, with a contained dignity, invited her five children for lunch and then quickly retreated to her bedroom, sat on the edge of her bed, and said goodbye to each of them. She told them her father had come to her during the night and told her that today would be the day. She laid her head on the pillows, and the last thing she said was, "I hear water falling." A few hours later she died, at ninety-six.

"The Procession"

Most of *In View of God* was concerned with two very important things for me. Does God exist? I wanted to believe in God so badly, but I had thrown over Catholicism.

When I was a young child, believing in God was mostly a matter of wanting to believe that God was a real person. I would often pray for God to give me a sign, a vision of affirmation as He gave to the saints, something to confirm my belief in Him. I was barely three weeks old when my parents, with the conviction of their faith, carried me to a Catholic church to have me baptized. It was in the same church, and I was held in the same arms of the same Italian priest who several years earlier married them. Of course I have no memory of this, but I was told, as I was told of so many things before I was born.

My parents were both very young when they immigrated to America from their small village in Sicily. They were children of peasant farmers, and all that their families brought with them was an innocent rural belief in God that had deep roots in the Sicilian soil they left behind. My mother was taught to pray seriously and privately, and she never prayed to anyone but the Blessed Virgin. My father, who never went to school, I think prayed to Jesus Christ, but I have few memories of ever seeing him in church. Their faith in God was a personal matter for each of them, and they had little consciousness of the church, with its religious regulations. Their belief in God was direct, and he was immediately there for them when they needed him. My mother raised me with her confident assumption that God was always with me because he had special love for children. But now when I try to remember, I had some doubts even then. Unfortunately I was a child with many questions.

When I was two years old, my mother, with some very good and strong arguments, convinced my father into moving the family to the north side of the city. She wanted to leave the old tenement district, which was a tight Italian community just west of downtown Chicago. The new neighborhood she chose had wide, quiet, clean streets, with rows of neatly kept bungalows and huge beautiful trees. "A perfect place," was the way my mother thought of it, for raising her children.

We were five children in my family, but I was the only boy. It was strange to grow up in a neighborhood where my family was the only Italian family. It separated my life by placing it into two very different worlds. Outside of my home, I had a free adventurous life, and prided myself with the feeling of independence. But inside my home, I felt tied to a continuous familiarity, a life that had defined a way of living and was connected to a pattern of behavior that existed for many years. There were excessive customs and old traditions that shaped my family, and they were always being kept alive by relatives and relatives of the relatives. I was told, and retold, quaint stories by expert storytellers. And there were wedding celebrations and funerals, and stifling afternoons with relentless holiday dinners. All this had to be endured because, I was told, "you're part of the family."

Every spring, down in the old Italian neighborhood, the Sicilians would celebrate the Feast of the Blessed Virgin. It always took place during the month of May, the month of the Virgin Mary. For this occasion the narrow streets in the tenement district would be brilliantly decorated with filigree arches of white lights, and Italian flags and banners draped over the banisters of the fire escapes. Endless rows of makeshift stalls, with vendors cooking and selling, would fill the air with the smells and smoke of exotic Sicilian foods. An enormous Ferris wheel strung with colored lights would take you up into the sky high above the buildings, so when you looked down you could see the dense crowds moving through the streets as a river would flow through a canyon. It was a village carnival, flavored with the traditions of the peasants, but at the edges, it was tinged with the harshness of urbanized poverty.

In contrast to the excitement and carnival spirit, the Feast of the Blessed Virgin for the Sicilian women was a very solemn and dark affair. For them it was a time to mourn and relive their sorrow. A time to commemorate the Virgin Mary for all her suffering, and for a long day of prayer. Beginning early in the morning right after sunrise, till late in the evening after sunset, they would follow the statue of the Virgin Mary holding her child as she was paraded through the streets on a high, ornate altar heavily decorated with flowers and hundreds of white candles.

The altar was attached to four very long poles and was carried by a group of young men in white pants and shirts wearing red bandannas tied tightly around their heads and silk red sashes around their waists. Up on the altar with the statue was the priest in his gold, brocaded robes and two teenage children dressed as angels, with delicately feathered wings strapped to their backs. When it was time for the procession to proceed, the priest would ring a bell and the men would hoist the poles of the altar onto their shoulders and run with it for several yards and then set it down on the pavement. Behind the altar followed a small band of wind instruments playing a slow funeral march, and behind them came the rows and rows and rows of women in black dresses carrying extremely large candles. When the altar was in place, the women would kneel down on the asphalt and pray with their rosary beads. While the women prayed, parents with infants would bring their child up to the altar so the child could kiss the Virgin statue. The parents would donate money to the church, and the angels would pin the money to a long cloak the statue was wearing, and by nightfall, the Virgin Mary would be wearing a garment covered in money.

At the end of the day, after the sun had disappeared behind the tenements, the procession would come to an end in front of the church, where the final ceremony would take place. In a dark sky, with floodlights shining down, you could see on the roof of two very tall tenement buildings, diagonally across from one another, two scaffold structures connected by long, thick ropes hanging over the street. Suddenly, without warning, out of the darkness would come the two angels descending from over the tops of the roofs, shouting and calling to the crowds below, "Silenzio, silenzio," and scattering rose petals from their baskets. Everyone on the street would go down on their knees.

As the ropes slackened, lowering the angels and leaving them suspended in the air slightly above the crown of the Virgin Mary, they would begin their plea of passion to the Holy Mother of God. Clenching their fists and biting their lips and extending their arms with the agony of two very dramatic actresses, they would speak of the pain and suffering the Virgin Mary endured when she was brought to see her son, Jesus Christ, crucified on the cross. They begged for her blessings and pleaded with her to forgive them for their sins, while the women below murmured and wept in unison like a Greek chorus. At the end of their plea the angels were instantly flown up to the tops of the buildings, disappearing from sight as if they had returned to heaven. An enormous explosion of fireworks would explode somewhere in a nearby street, with the sound reverberating off the buildings. In astonishment, I always found myself holding my breath.

One year my mother made a promise to the Virgin Mary that she would walk in the procession and pray for her to help my sister Margaret overcome a very serious illness. I was anxious about her decision, because I knew how uncomfortable it would be for me to see my mother walking in the streets with all the other women. For most of that day I followed along the side of the procession, holding back my tears, keeping my eyes on her alone. I went down with her when she knelt in the street on both her knees and prayed with her rosary beads twisting through her fingers. She always kept her eyes averted and never seemed to notice that I was standing on the curb just a few feet away from her. With her head bowed, holding her melting candle, she looked so ancient. Her appearance was so foreign, and I felt such a distance separating us.

Riverview

Riverview Amusement Park was less than a mile from where I lived. It was built sometime during the late nineteenth century and appeared to have remained virtually unchanged since then. In a slight state of nostalgic decay, it spread five or six miles along the banks of the Chicago River. It was considered to be the world's largest amusement park.

In the late thirties and early forties, just after the Second World War had started, the park was always swarming with rowdy sailors and soldiers on leave. The Western Avenue streetcar, which ran along the front of the park, would bring carload after carload of very poor, but very excitable, young black people from the south side of the city. During the summer months, and for the last years of the Great Depression, the park would draw tremendous crowds.

My father, who enjoyed the park as much as I did, would take me there when I was very young, but this was not a place for children. Riverview was not a Disneyland with a clean, controlled, synthetic environment. You could feel the grime on the surface of everything from years of unseemly, reckless entertainment.

There were five world-famous roller coasters and a variety of gambling booths with card games and dice. For the winners there was a splendid array of garishly decorated prizes. There were also loud shooting galleries with shotguns and pistols for the bullets to shatter dinner plates and bottles, and there was even a game with a sledgehammer for the muscle men to swing with all their violent power, slamming it down on an iron scale that measured the power of their blow.

But the game that intrigued the men the most, particularly the tough, aggressive white males, was a game with a row of tall steel cages with a black man in each cage, wearing a gray rubber suit and sitting up on a metal bar yelling obscenities to the men standing on the outside. For a dime, the provoked angry white males could buy three hard balls to throw at a small red disk extended out the side of each cage. If they hit the disk, the bar inside the cage would break in half and the black man would drop down, plunging into a large wooden tub filled with water. With all the cursing and angry name-calling going back and forth between the men, a crowd of spectators always gathered to cheer and applaud whenever a black man plunged into the water.

When I was old enough to go to the park alone I would go there for hours to mingle with the crowds while I meandered around. I had an insatiable curiosity, and I was as fascinated as a Peeping Tom. I was at an age when watching grown-ups enjoy themselves, unleashing their pleasures in outrageous ways, was an exciting pastime.

Every summer the park always had a freak show, Ripley's "Believe It or Not." One year, with top billing, the featured attraction was the Frog Boy: a boy who was supposedly born with the body of a frog. I always felt a little hesitant, or I should say scared, to go in and actually look at the freaks. But seeing the big poster painted on the front of the building of a boy with the body of a frog piqued my imagination, so I timidly, but excitedly, bought a ticket and went in.

After going through a dimly lighted passageway I found myself in a room, standing on a balcony looking down into a pit. On the floor at the bottom of the pit was scattered sawdust and some small, peculiar objects, which I think were there for him to play with. At first I thought he wasn't there, but then I saw him at the far side of the pit crouched in a corner chewing on a scrap of food. He was busy eating, so he hadn't noticed that I entered the room. The sight of him was almost too painful for me to look at him. He was excruciatingly thin, his lower body, emaciated to the point of being crippled. He was wearing a pair of shabby green tights with black spots painted on them. His deformity was tragic, and he looked tortured in the horrible condition of his humiliating situation.

When he looked up and saw me he stopped eating, and then with his legs buckled up under his torso he awkwardly, with a hopping kind of movement, came over to the side of the pit where I was standing looking down. For a moment he blinked his very large, dark eyes, and then with a look, so penetratingly clear, so intelligently human, he stared directly up at me. I realized he was an aware young boy, about my own age, with a normal mind, who was about to speak to me. I immediately stepped backward away from the railing, out of his sight. In my mind I was no longer there; shaking, I left the room. I had many restless nights after that, trying to grasp my awful feeling of guilt. I knew then that there was so much that I didn't understand and couldn't answer.

> The human condition is not only pain.
> Yet pain rules us and has much power.
> Wise thoughts fail us in its presence.
> Starry skies go out.
> —Czeslaw Milosz

Appendix B

A Chronology of Works by Paul Sanasardo, Donya Feuer, and Studio for Dance Productions, 1954–2002

This chronology has been pieced together from many different sources. Sometimes it was not possible to ascertain the exact day or month of a première; in such cases the entry gives only the information that is known.

December 12, 1954, Educational Alliance, New York

Feuer, *With Love* (Scarlatti), *Vigil* (Webern), *Two Songs* (Brunner), *In Dreams Begin Responsibility*

February 24, 1955, 92nd Street Y, New York

Sanasardo, perf., Anna Sokolow, *Rooms* (Hopkins)

Sanasardo subsequently danced in the following Sokolow works: Poem, Lyric Suite, Metamorphosis (*an early study for* Opus Jazz), The Seven Deadly Sins, The Moon, L'Histoire du soldat, *in Sokolow's choreography for the Broadway musical* Candide *and the Broadway play* Red Roses for Me, *and at the New York City Opera in Sokolow's choreography for* Orpheus in the Underworld, La Traviata, The Tempest, *and* Susannah. *During this period he also appeared in Donald McKayle's* Nocturne *and was seen on television in* "Lamp unto my Feet" *and* "Omnibus" *in choreography by John Butler and Mary Anthony.*

April 26, 1955, Master Institute, New York

Feuer, *Remembrance of the Moon* (J. S. Bach), *I'll Be You and You Be Me* (Rameau)

As a member of the Martha Graham Dance Company, Feuer performed Night Journey, Appalachian Spring, *and* Diversion of Angels *on the Asian tour, October 1955–February 1956.*

June 5, 1956, Master Institute (under sponsorship of Dance Associates), New York
Feuer, *Chamber Music* (Couperin, Marin, Soler)
Sanasardo, *Three Dances of Death in the Grand Manner* (Chopin, Liszt, Ravel)

April 8, 1957, Rooftop Theatre, New York
Feuer, *A Serious Dance for Three Fools* (Johnson)
Sanasardo, *A Dance Adaptation of Gertrude Stein's "Doctor Faustus Lights the Lights"* (Wuorinen, original score)
In 1957 Sanasardo danced Sokolow's choreography in Shirley Clarke's film A Moment in Love. *He performed from 1957 until 1965 with Pearl Lang in her* Apasionada, Rites, Shoreborne, Dichotomy, Shirah, And Joy Is My Witness, The Possessed (The Dybbuk), Broken Dialogues, Archaic Prelude, *and* Legend.

October 20, 1957, 92nd Street Y, New York
Feuer, perf., Paul Taylor, *Seven New Dances* (Cage)
Feuer also danced Taylor's Three Epitaphs.

February 22, 1958, Henry Street Playhouse, New York
Feuer, *Dust for Sparrows* (Webern, de Falla)
Sanasardo, *Because of Love* (Villa Lobos)

1959, Studio for Dance, New York
Judith Blackstone, *Afraid of the Dark* (Debussy)
Willa Kahn, *Want* (Ravel)
Blackstone and Kahn, *Where Do We Come From, What Are We, Where Are We Going* (Rimsky-Korsakov)

May 2, 1959, 92nd Street Y, New York
Sanasardo and Feuer, *In View of God* (Ginastera, Blomdahl)

Spring 1960, tour of New York City Public Schools with Arthur Weisberg's Contemporary Chamber Ensemble
Sanasardo, Feuer, and Pina Bausch, *Three Phases of Madness* (Varèse)

May 29, 1960, Henry Street Playhouse, New York ("a dance program for early personalities")

Sanasardo, *I'll Be You and You Be Me* (Rameau)

Ruth Frank, *What Do We Seek*

Kahn, *Presence* (Bartok)

Blackstone, *House of Tattered Symbols* (Kodaly)

Feuer, *Dust for Sparrows* (Webern, de Falla)

I'll Be You and You Be Me *and* Dust for Sparrows *in versions rechoreographed for the children.*

June 18, 1960, Hunter Playhouse, New York
Sanasardo and Feuer, *Laughter after All* (Varèse)

May 14, 1961, 92nd Street Y, New York
Sanasardo and Feuer, *Pictures in Our House* (music in public domain)

October 14 and 15, 1961, Hunter Playhouse, New York
Sanasardo and Feuer, *Excursion for Miracles* (in two parts)
(Mossolov, Ussachevsky, Dodds, Russell, Schaeffer, Badings, Henry, Raajmakers, Cowell, Rodan)

1962
Bausch returns to Germany

February 8, 1963, Hunter Playhouse, New York
Sanasardo and Feuer, *Of Human Kindness* (Finckel, original score)
Sanasardo, *Opulent Dream* (Scriaben)

February 12, 1963
Feuer leaves for Stockholm

Spring 1963, Midwestern tour to Minnesota, Missouri, North Dakota, and South Dakota
Sanasardo, *Metallics* (Cowell, Badings), *Two Movements for Strings* (Ginastera)

Metallics *was re-staged for the Alvin Ailey Dance Company, the First Chamber Dance Quartet, the Netherlands Dance Theatre, Bat Dor, the Winnepeg Repertory Company, and John Passafiume Dancers.*

August 1, 1963, Park Teatern, Stockholm
Feuer, *Angels by Chance* (with Bruce Marks and Vevka Ljung) (Björlin), *Ekon* (*Echo*) (Björlin)

Performed with Birgit Cullberg's Seven Deadly Sins. Angels by Chance *and* Ekon *were debuts for Mats Ek and Niklas Ek.*

October 5, 1963, Judson Hall, New York

Diane Germaine, *Trichotomy* (Richter), *Pastel* (Cage), *Monody*
(Varèse)

Manuel Alum, *Of Wings I Lack* (Colgrass), *Familial Trio* (Badings)

Blackstone, *Shell to Shelter—Shell to Break* (Buxtehude)

December 1963, Statsteatern, Upsala

Feuer, chor., Shakespeare, *Öthello* (*Othello*) (Frank Sundström, dir.)

December 12, 1963, Dramaten, Stockholm

Feuer, perf., John Gay, *Tiggarens Opera* (*The Beggar's Opera*) (Per-
Axel Branner, dir.)

February 1, 1964, Hunter Playhouse, New York

Sanasardo, *Laughter after All* (revised version) (Varèse, Syrjala)

February 28, 1964, Kungliga Dramatiska Teatern (Dramaten),
Stockholm

Feuer, chor., Jean Genet, *Balkongen* (*The Balcony*) (Frank Sundström,
dir.) (Björlin)

March 10, 1964, Dramaten, Stockholm

Feuer, *Hjärtat & revbenet* (*The Heart and the Rib*) (Björlin), an
evening of chamber music and dance presented by Ingmar
Bergman

*This production inaugurated a long collaboration between Feuer, Bergman,
composer Ulf Björlin, and costume and set designer Lennart Mörk.*

April 1964, Oscarteatern, Stockholm

Feuer, chor. and perf., Luigi Pirandello, *Jättarna på berget* (*Giants on
the Mountain*) (Frank Sundström, dir.)

April 25, 1964, Stadsteatern, Stockholm

Feuer, chor. and perf., *Självporträtt I: ragtime för en princessa* (*Selfportrait I: Ragtime for a Princess*) (Stravinsky); dir., Samuel
Beckett, *Akt utan ord* (*Act without Words*)

May 8, 1964, Stadsteatern, Upsala

Feuer, chor., *Ärkänglar spelar inte falsk* (*Archangels Do Not Cheat*)

October 1964, Dramaten, Stockholm

Feuer, chor., Witold Gombrowicz, *Yvonne, princessa av Burgund*
(*Yvonne, Princess of Burgundy*) (Alf Sjöberg, dir.)

Feuer's first collaboration with Alf Sjöberg.

October 31, 1964, 92nd Street Y, New York
Sanasardo, *Forward in the Dark* (Kodaly), *Pictures in Our House*
(revised version; music in public domain)

April 5, 1965, Dramaten, Stockholm
Feuer, chor., Peter Weiss, *Mordet på Marat* (*Marat-Sade*) (Frank
Sundström, dir.)

December 2, 1965, Historiska Museet, Stockholm
Feuer, *Spel för museet* (*A Play for a Museum*) (Björlin, original score)

January 22, 1966, Stadsteatern, Stockholm
Feuer, *Att dansa* (*To Dance*) (Björlin, original score), *En romantisk
balett* (*A Romantic Ballet*) (Zimmerman)

January 29, 1966, 92nd Street Y, New York
Sanasardo, *Fatal Birds* (Ginastera), *An Earthly Distance* (Henry),
The Animal's Eye (Schoenberg)

February 26, 1966, 92nd Street Y, New York
Alum, *The Offering* (Penderecki), *Storm* (Luciuk), *Nightbloom*
(Serocki)
Blackstone, *Broken Voyage* (Vivaldi)
Germaine, *Recurring Dream* (Varèse, Dockstader)
Barbara Dolgin, *Breakthrough* (Stanley Walden, original score)

March 26, 1966, 92nd Street Y, New York
Works by Elina Mooney, Cliff Keuter, and Sally Bowden

April 30, 1966, 92nd Street Y, New York
Sanasardo, *Excursions* (Lester; Syrjala, original score)

December 17, 1966, 92nd Street Y
Sanasardo, *Cut Flowers* (Serocki), *Early Darkness* (revised version of
Forward in the Dark) (Kodaly)

December 18, 1966, Dramaten, Stockholm
Feuer, chor., Witold Gombrowicz, *Vigseln* (*The Wedding*) (Alf
Sjöberg, dir.) (Björlin, original score)

January 25, 1967, 92nd Street Y, New York
Germaine, *One Other One* (Sydeman)
Bowden, *Continuum* (Greene)
Franko, *The Confidence* (Hindemith)

February 28, 1967, 92nd Street Y, New York
  Sanasardo, *Limited Edition* (Sanasardo) (with improvised
    percussion)
  Germaine, *The Moth* (Vivaldi)
  Blackstone, *The Vision* (Chavez)

March 10, 1967, Dramaten, Stockholm
  Feuer, chor., Staffan Roos, *Cirkus Madigan* (*Madigan's Circus*)
    (Staffan Roos, dir.)

March 22, 1967, 92nd Street Y, New York
  Sanasardo, *Three Dances* (Paul Knopf, original score)
  Bowden, *Collection* (Greene)
  Alum, *Fantasía* (Hamilton)

May 21, 1967, Dramaten, Stockholm
  Feuer, chor., Shakespeare, *Troilus och Cressida* (*Troilus and Cressida*)
    (Alf Sjöberg, dir.) (Björlin, original score)

June 1967, Festival of Two Worlds, Spoleto, Italy
  Alum, *The Cellar* (Kilar)

August 1967, Spa Summer Theatre, Saratoga, New York
  Alum, chor. *Dream after Dream and After* (Johnson)

September 2, 1967, Dramaten, Stockholm
  Feuer, chor. and dir., Shakespeare, *En midsommarnattsdröm*
    (*A Midsummer Night's Dream*)

October 27, 1967, Dramaten, Stockholm
  Feuer, dir. and chor., Federico Garcia Lorca, *Om fem år* (*If Five Years
    Pass: An Opera for Actors*) (Björlin, original score)

November 5, 1967, Stadsteatern, Stockholm
  Feuer, *Love Love Love* (performed by Cullberg Ballet) (psychedelic
    pop)

December 2, 1967, Sveriges Television (SVT, Swedish Television),
    Stockholm
  Feuer, *Ett spel om föremål och människor* (*A Play of Objects and People*)
    (Björlin)
  The television version of A Play for a Museum.

April 4, 1968, Dramaten, Stockholm
Feuer, chor., Euripides, *Alkestis* (*Alcestis*) (Alf Sjöberg, dir.) (Björlin)

May 15, 1968, Hunter Playhouse, New York
Sanasardo, *The Descent* (Maderna)
Alum, *Palomas* (Oliveros)

Palomas *originally set on Elizabeth Rockwell's Northern Westchester Dance Company, and later performed by Bat Dor, Israel. The original subtitle was A Lament of the Young in a Time of War.*

June 8, 1968, Dramaten, Stockholm
Feuer, chor., *Fem på Dramaten* (*Five at Dramaten*)
Feuer and four invited choreographers present a concert of new works.

August 1968, Spa Summer Theater, Saratoga, New York
Alum, *Dream and Trial* (Luciuk)

November 2, 1968, Dramaten, Stockholm
Feuer, dir., Shakespeare, *Stormen* (*The Tempest*)

January 11, 1969, Dramaten, Stockholm
Feuer, dir., Friedrich Schiller, *Don Carlos* (*Don Carlos*), with Staffan Roos (Björlin, original score)

February 20, 1969, Dramaten, Stockholm
Feuer, chor., Arne Tornquist, *Carl XVI Joseph* (*Carl Joseph XVI*) (Mimi Pollack, dir.)

March 22, 1969, Sveriges Television, Stockholm
Feuer, *Himlakropp* (*Heavenly Body*) (Björlin, original score)

April 5, 1969, Sveriges Television, Stockholm
Feuer, perf. (as the Hexin), Eske Holm, chor., *Bikt* (*Confession*), with Anders Ek and Niklas Ek

April 11, 1969, Dramaten, Stockholm
Feuer, chor., Bertolt Brecht, *Tollvskillingsoperan* (*Threepenny Opera*) (Alf Sjöberg, dir.) (Weil)

June 1, 1969, Hunter Playhouse, New York
Sanasardo, *Pain* (Lutoslawski)

June 7, 1969, Hunter Playhouse, New York
Alum, *Overleaf* (Messiaen)

September 25, 1969, Dramaten, Stockholm
Feuer, dir. and chor., Elias Canetti, *Bröllopsfesten* (*The Wedding Party*)

October 21, 1969, Trondheim, Norway
Feuer, *Under pausen* (*During the Intermission*), performed by Cullberg Ballet (no music)

December 7, 1969, Delacorte Theatre, New York
Sanasardo, *Earth* (Gerhard), performed by Repertory Dance Theater of Utah

1970, Tröndelags Teater, Tröndelag, Norway
Feuer, dir. and chor., Federico Garcia Lorca, *Bernardas Hus* (*The House of Bernarda Alba*)
Followed by a tour of Norway.

1970, Norska Operan (Norwegian Opera), Oslo
Feuer, *Aft Vaemod* (*To the Memory of Vämod*) (Björlin)

May 14, 1970, City Center, New York
Sanasardo, *Footnotes* (Eugene Lester, original score)
Made possible by a grant from the Guggenheim Foundation. The Paul Sanasardo Dance Company tours to Bermuda, Puerto Rico, and Nassau in the late sixties, and under Hurok Management and through the National Endowment touring program throughout the United States in the seventies.

May 20, 1970, Dramaten, Stockholm
Feuer, dir., *Verligheter: tre kortpjäser* (*Realities: Three Short Plays*); Samuel Beckett, *Från eyy övergivet arbete* (*From an Abandoned Work*), Harold Pinter, *Landskap* (*Lanscape*), *Om natten* (*The Homecoming*)

November 21, 1970, 92nd Street Y, New York
Alum, *Era* (Penderecki), *Roly-Poly* (Berio)

December 18, 1970, Dramaten, Stockholm
Feuer, chor. and dir., Federico Garcia Lorca, *Blodsbröllop* (*Blood Wedding*) (Björlin, original score)

1971, Historiska Museet, Stockholm
Feuer, *Varg rop* (*The Howling of Wolves*), with Diane Germaine (to recorded wolf howling)

March 9, 1971, Moderna Museet, Stockholm
  Feuer, *Dans på utställning* (*Dance for the Gallery*) (Björlin)

March 20, 1971, Dramaten, Stockholm
  Feuer, chor. and perf., Lars Forsell, *Show* (Ingmar Berman, dir.)
    (Werle)
  The first performance involving Dans Kompaniet, which continues until 1976.

April 24, 1971, Dramaten, Stockholm
  Feuer, *Gud lever och har hälsan* (*God Is Alive and in Fairly Good Health*)
    (Joplin, Riley, Henry)
  *The ballet was set on the Paul Sanasardo Dance Company in June–July 1971; in the
    version performed by the Norwegian Ballet, Oslo, in 1975, the subtitle is* That
    Love Is All, Is All We Know of Love.

April 29, 1971, Schenectady Museum, New York (WHMT-TV)
  Sanasardo and Alum, *Cyclometry* (Serocki, Penderecki, Lutoslowski)
  A restaging of Cut Flowers, Era, *and* Pain.

May 20, 1971, Brooklyn Academy of Music, New York
  Sanasardo, *Sight Seeing* (Eugene Lester, original score)

June 1971, Seattle Playhouse, Oregon
  Sanasardo, *The Myth,* performed by the First Chamber Dance
    Quartet (Kodaly)

August 1971, Spa Summer Theatre, Saratoga, New York
  Feuer, *God Is Alive and in Fairly Good Health* (Joplin, Riley, Henry)
  *The ballet is performed again in Stockholm on September 15, 1971, with Alum in
    the role of God.*

November, 1971, Bat-Dor Dance Company, Tel Aviv
  Sanasardo, *Voices* (Serocki)
  Sanasardo also staged Metallics *during this visit.*

1972, Norsk Rikskingkasting (NRK, Norwegian Television), Oslo
  Feuer, dir., films *Ett syn* (*The Vision*); *Frukõst* (*Breakfast*), *Med Kroppen
    som ensats* (*With the Body as Downpayment*)

January 6, 1972, Sveriges Television, Stockholm
  Feuer, chor. and dir., *Taxinge-Näsby Station: fantasi för TV* (with
    Manuel Alum)

May 5, 1972, Dramaten, Stockholm
Feuer, chor., August Strindberg, *Mäster Olof* (Alf Sjöberg, dir.)
(Björlin, original score)

August 13, 1972, Spa Summer Theatre, Saratoga, New York
Sanasardo, *The Path* (Drews)

August 20, 1972, Spa Summer Theatre, Saratoga, New York
Bausch, *Philips 836887 DSY* (Henry); *Nachnull* (*After Zero*) (Malek)
Alum, *Sextetrahedron* (Borden)

August 26, 1972, Spa Summer Theatre, Saratoga, New York
Alum, *Woman of Mystic Body* (Verdi) (a solo for Malou Airaudo)
Germaine, *Stop-Over* (Watson)
Sanasardo, *Romance* (Barr)

October 1972, Bat-Dor Dance Company, Tel Aviv
Sanasardo, *A Little Hell* (Haidu)
Sanasardo also staged The Myth *during this visit.*

December 12, 1972, Dramaten, Stockholm
Feuer, chor., Peter Weiss, *Hölderlin* (Lars Göran Carlsson, dir.)

1973, Tröndelags Teater, Tröndelag, Norway
Feuer, dir. and chor., Dario Fo, *Anarkistens Död* (*The Death of an
Anarchist*)

March 23, 1973, Dramaten, Stockholm
Feuer, chor., Carlo Goldoni, *Gruffet I Chiozza* (Alf Sjöberg, dir.)
(Björlin)

April 1973, Exchange Theatre, New York
Sanasardo, *Small Prayers* (Drago, Pipo, Ohana, Pujol)

April 23, 1973, Exchange Theatre, New York
Sanasardo, *Shadows* (Satie, Scarlatti, Bach)
*Also performed by Bat Dor, Winnepeg Repertory Company, and John Passafiume
Dancers.*

June 1973, Sveriges Television, Stockholm
Feuer, chor., *De fördörnde Kvinnornas Dans* (*Ballo delle Ungrate—
Dance of the Ungrateful Women*) (Ingmar Bergman, dir.)
(Monteverdi)
A dance-film experiment shot by Sven Nykvist at Farö.

October 1973, Bat-Dor Dance Company, Tel Aviv
  Sanasardo, *Carnival* (Vivaldi)
  Sanasardo also staged Shadows *during this visit.*

November 22, 1973, Dramaten, Stockholm
  Feuer, chor. and dir., Lars Norén, *Fursteslickaren* (*The Prince's
    Asslicker*) (Björn Lindh)

1974, Norsk Rikskingkasting (NRK, Norwegian Television), Oslo
  Feuer, chor., *Farväl* (*Farewell: Variations on the Romeo-Juliet theme*)

1974, Tröndelags Teater, Tröndelag, Norway
  Feuer, dir. and chor., Donya Feuer based on A. A. Milne, *Nalle Puh*
    (*Winnie the Pooh*)

1974, Sveriges Television, Stockholm
  Feuer, chor. and dir., Lars Norén, *Livet är den tid det tar mig att dö*
    (*Life Is the Time That It Takes Me to Die*)
  *Based on poems written by Norén for this production. The film was destroyed in
    the SVT archive.*

1974, Norsk Rikskingkasting, Oslo
  Feuer, dir., in cooperation with Romola Nijinsky, documentary film
    Ett liv (*A Life*); Feuer, chor. and dir., film *Requiem för en dansare*
    (*Requiem for a Dancer*)
  These two films were shown together with a short intermission between.

February 1974, Gulbenkian Ballet, Lisbon
  Sanasardo, *O baile dos mendigos* (*The Beggar's Ballroom*) (Beethoven)

May 18–24, 1974, Brooklyn Academy of Music, New York
  Sanasardo, *Platform* (Bach)
  Sokolow, *Equatorial* (Varèse)

July 9, 1974, Dennis Wayne's American Ballet Company, Jacob's Pillow
    Dance Festival
  Sanasardo, *A Sketch for Donna* (Bach)

October 1974, Detroit Dance, Detroit, Michigan
  Sanasardo, *Disappearances*

December 14, 1974, Dramaten, Stockholm
  Feuer, chor., Bertolt Brecht, *Galilei* (*Galileo*) (Alf Sjöberg, dir.)
    (Eisler)

December 29, 1974, American Theatre Laboratory, New York
Sanasardo, *The Amazing Graces* (Dvorak)

1974–1977, Statens Musikdramatiska Skola (State Dramatic Music
School), Stockholm
Feuer, dir. and chor. operas, including Britten, *The Rape of Lucretia*,
Mozart, *The Mariage of Figaro*, Händel, *Xerxes*, and Orff, *Die Kluge*.

1975, Ballet Théâtre Contemporain d'Angers, Théâtre de la Ville, Paris
Sanasardo, *Saints and Lovers* (Mayuzumi)

Spring 1975, Bat-Dor Dance Company, Tel Aviv
Sanasardo, *Sketches for Nostalgic Children* (Gottshalk); *Pearl River*

April 28, 1975, Dramaten, Stockholm
Feuer, chor., Shakespeare, *Tretttondagsafton eller vad ni behager*
(*Twelfth Night*) (Ingmar Bergman, dir.) (Björlin)

June 25, 1975, City Center Theater, New York
Sanasardo, *A Consort for Dancers* (text by Ann Sexton read by
Marion Winter and William Weaver; music improvised in
performance by Gwendolyn Watson)
Made possible by a grant from the National Endowment for the Arts.

October 1975, Svenska Filminstitutet, Stockholm
Feuer, chor., Mozart, *Trollflötten* (Ingmar Bergman's film version of
The Magic Flute)

December 9, 1975, City Center Downstairs, New York
Sanasardo, *A Memory Suite* (Thomson, Clarke, Simon, Hohne)

1976, Norwegian Film, Oslo
Feuer, dir., documentary film *Victor Rona—the Artist*

February 28, 1976, Royal Swedish Opera, Tecnorama, Stockholm
Feuer, chor. and dir., *Gilgamesh* (Nörgard)

September 12, 1976, New York Shakespeare Festival, Delacorte
Theater, New York
Sanasardo, *Andantino cantabile* (Enescu) (duet for Lawrence Rhodes
and Naomi Sorkin)

December 17, 1976, Shepard Great Hall, City College of New York
Sanasardo, *Abandoned Prayer* (Albinoni)

1977, Stadsteatern, Malmö (opera production)
  Feuer, chor., *Aniara* (Blomdahl)

1977, Batsheva Dance Company, Tel Aviv
  Sanasardo, *Step by Step with Hayden* (Hayden)

1977, Dennis Wayne Dancers, Roundabout Theatre, New York
  Sanasardo, *Romantic Realm* (Wagner)

1977, Atlanta Contemporary Dance Company, Atlanta, Georgia
  Sanasardo, *Ocean Beach*

1977, Rhode Island Dance Repertory Company, Providence
  Sanasardo, *Providence*

June 14, 1977, Roundabout Theatre, New York
  Sanasardo, *Triad* (Crumb)
  William Carter, *Of Silent Doors and Sunsets* (Beethoven)
  Triad *made for Naomi Sorkin.*

November 29, 1977, Theater Carré, Dutch Opera with Concertgebouw
    Orchestra, Amsterdam
  Feuer, dir., Adrian Mitchell, *Houdini: A Circus Opera* (Schat) (world
    première)

March 2, 1978, Dramaten, Stockholm
  Feuer, dir., Donya Feuer based on Ted Hughes's *A Choice of
    Shakespeare's verse, Pejlingar* (*Soundings*) ("Soliloquy" for Karin
    Kavli)
  The first performance in an ongoing collaboration with Ted Hughes.

March 25, 1978, Batsheva Dance Company, Tel Aviv
  Sanasardo, *Lisztdelerium* (Liszt); *Meditations on an Open Stage* (Avni)

September 1, 1978, Dramaten, Stockholm
  Feuer, dir., *Klassikerstormen* (*Classic Tempest*)
  Versions of nuclear disaster with other directors.

1979, Tröndelags Teater, Tröndelag, Norway
  Feuer, dir. and chor., Shakespeare, *Öthello* (*Othello*) (version by Kjell
    Stormoen)

December, 1979, Joel Hall Dancers, Chicago
  Sanasardo, *Territories* (Stravinsky)

January 8, 1980, Dramaten, Stockholm

Feuer, dir., author unknown, *Kvinnors liv och kärlek* (*Women's Life and Love*) (Schubert)

January 26, 1979, Dramaten, Stockholm

Feuer, chor. and dir., Shakespeare, *Lika för lika* (*Measure for Measure*)

1980, Israeli Television, Tel Aviv

Sanasardo, *Babi-Yar* (Shostakovich)

Included footage of interviews with early settlers that disappeared before broadcast.

February 14, 1980, Schimmel Center, Pace University, New York

Sanasardo, *Time No More,* performed by Joan Lombardi Dancers (Messiaen)

1980, Göte Lejon, Stockholm

Feuer, dir. and chor., *Månen* (*The Moon*), with Stockholms Musik Dramatiska Ensemble (Orff)

March 1980, Batsheva Dance Company, Habima Theater, Tel Aviv

Sanasardo, *Songs—From Jewish Folk Poetry* (Shostakovitch)

During his tenure as director of Batsheva Dance Company, Sanasardo also tours nationally and internationally with a repertory that includes works by Kurt Jooss, David Hatch Walker, Rahamim Ron, Matthew Diamond, John Cranko, Donald McKayle, Norbert Vesak, Yair Vardi, Glen Tetley, and Valery Panov, as well as his own Abandoned Prayer *and* Step by Step *with Hayden.*

March 1980, Mann Auditorium, Tel Aviv

Sanasardo, *The Stravinsky Rotating Dance Circus* (Stravinsky)

Commissioned by the Israeli Philharmonic Orchestra.

April 9, 1980, Dramaten, Stockholm

Feuer, chor., Molière, *Hustruskolan* (*School for Wives*) (Alf Sjöberg, dir.)

September 13, 1980, Fakt Theater, Amsterdam

Feuer, dir. *Ank Van Der Moeur Plays Shakespeare*

A version of Soundings.

1981, Cornish Dance Theater, Seattle, Oregon

Sanasardo, *Forget Me Not*

1981, Kulturhuset, Stockholm
  Feuer, dir., *Samuel Beckett: Eighty Years*

1981, Chicago Repertory Dance Ensemble, Chicago
  Sanasardo, *Solo from the Blue Window* (Bach)

1981, Cleo Parker Robinson Dance, Denver Opera, Denver
  Sanasardo, *Sunset-Sunrise* (Copland)

March 7, 1981, Dramaten, Stockholm
  Feuer, dir., August Strindberg, *Päsk* (*Easter*)

March 28, 1982, Dramaten, Stockholm
  Feuer, dir., Sam Shepard, *Action*

April 30, 1981, Dramaten, Stockholm
  Feuer, dir. and chor., Solveig Ternström, *Vi ses i Berlin* (*We'll Meet in Berlin*)

October 2, 1981, Dramaten, Stockholm
  Feuer, chor., Per Olof Enquist, *Frän Regnormamas Liv* (*From the Life of a Rainsnake*)

May 11, 1982, City Center Space, New York
  Sanasardo, *The Abiding Void* (Violette)

May 20, 1982, City Center Space, New York
  Sanasardo, *Miniatures* (Beethoven)

May 30, 1982, City Center Space, New York
  Sanasardo, *The Blue Window* (Bach)

1983, The Egg, Albany, New York
  Sanasardo, *Premonitions* (Ives, Milhaud, Skalkottus)

1984, Norska Operan, Oslo
  Feuer, *En svanesäng* (*A Swan's Song*) (Mahler, Schumann)

March 9, 1984, Dramaten, Stockholm
  Feuer, chor., Shakespeare, *Kung Lear* (*King Lear*) (Ingmar Bergman, dir.)
  Bergman's first production after his return from exile in Germany.

May 16, 1984, Riverside Dance Festival, New York
  Sanasardo, *La ronde des femmes* (Poulenc); *Children in the Mist* (Bartok)

January 24, 1985, Dramaten, Stockholm
Feuer, chor., Shakespeare, *Julius Caesar* (Staffan Roos, dir.)

August 24, 1985, Dramaten, Stockholm
Feuer, chor. and dir., from the *Duino Elegies* of Rainer Maria Rilke, *Ej blot til lyst* (*Not Just as an Amusement*) (Bach)

1986, Binghamton Ballet Company, New York
Sanasardo, *Scattered Clouds* (Satie)

March 19, 1986, Riverside Dance Festival, New York
Sanasardo, *Mysteries* (collage)

February 12, 1987, Royal Swedish Opera, Stockholm
Feuer, chor. and dir., Tormud Haugen *Slottet det vita* (*The White Castle*) (Sandström)
The first performances in 1986 were done as chamber music versions.

1987, Symphony Hall, San Diego
Sanasardo, perf., Charles Bennett, *Dracula* (with the California Ballet Company)

1987, Emma Willard Company, Schenectady, New York
Sanasardo, *Street Scene*

1988, Stockholm
Feuer, dir., *Vem är Hill?* (*Who Is Hill?*)

April 9, 1988, Kulturhuset, Stockholm
Feuer, dir. and chor., Doris Lessing, *En Overlevandes Minnen: ett Forskningsprojekt för teater av Donya Feuer* (*Memoirs of a Survivor: an Investigation in Theater by Donya Feuer*).
With Gunnel Lindblom and fifty school children. The idea was suggested and the manuscript prepared by Sonya Feuer Bemporad.

December 31, 1988, Dramaten, Stockholm
Feuer, dir., with Agne Pauli, *På Håret-Revyn* (*Last-Minute Revue*)

April 7, 1989, Dramaten, Stockholm
Feuer, chor., Yukio Mishima, *Markisinnan de Sade* (*Marquis de Sade*) (Ingmar Bergman, dir.)
Performed at the Brooklyn Academy of Music, New York, June 7–10, 1995.

November 4, 1989, Dramaten, Stockholm
> Feuer, dir., Kristina Lugn, *Det vackra blir liksom över* (*What Is Beautiful Gets Left Over*)

November 17, 1989, Dramaten, Stockholm
> Feuer, chor., Henrik Ibsen, *Ett dockhem* (*A Doll's House*) (Ingmar Bergman, dir.)

1991, Kulturhuset, Stockholm
> Feuer, dir., Ted Hughes, *More Than Cool Reason Ever Comprehends*
>
> *The first production of* In the Company of Shakespeare. *Ted Hughes's version of* the Midsummer Night's Dream *for "N3B."*

1991, Sveriges Television, Stockholm
> Feuer, perf., Per Jönsson, *Three Dances*

April 22, 1991, Dramaten, Stockholm
> Feuer, chor., Henrik Ibsen, *Peer Gynt* (Ingmar Bergman, dir.) (Martinu)
>
> *Performed at the Brooklyn Academy of Music, New York, May 11–15, 1993.*

November 2, 1991, Royal Swedish Opera, Stockholm
> Feuer, chor., opera based on Euripedes, *Backanterna* (*The Bacchae*) (Ingmar Bergman, dir.) (Börtz)

1992, Sveriges Television, Stockholm
> Feuer, chor., television version of the opera *Backanterna* (*The Bacchae*) (Ingmar Bergman, dir.)

April 4, 1992, Dramaten, Stockholm
> Feuer, chor., Hans Alfredson, *Dödgrären* (*Gravedigger*) (Jan-Olof Strandberg, dir.)

June 1, 1992, Kulturhuset, Stockholm
> Feuer, dir., Donya Feuer, *In a Dream of Passion*
>
> *Based on Ted Hughes's* A Choice of Shakespeare's Verse.

April 22, 1993, Kulturhuset, Stockholm
> Feuer, dir., Donya Feuer, *As If We Were God's Spies*
>
> *Based on Ted Hughes's* A Choice of Shakespeare's Verse.

September 30, 1993, the Fourteenth Festival of Poetry, Sibiu, Roumania
> Feuer, dir., Donya Feuer, *When My Cue Comes*
>
> *Based on Ted Hughes's* A Choice of Shakespeare's Verse.

October 3, 1993, Dramaten, Stockholm
Feuer, dir., *Bottens dröm* (*Bottom's Dream*)
Based on Ted Hughes's A Choice of Shakespeare's Verse.

1994, Berlin Film Festival, Berlin
Feuer, dir., film *Dansaren* (*The Dancer*)
With Katja Björner, Anneli Alhanko, and Erland Josephson. New York première at the "Dance on Film" Festival, Walter Reade Theater, December 1–7, 1995. Dansaren was nominated for an Academy Award; best Nordic documentary (1994); Certificate of Merit Winner, Golden Gate Award (San Francisco, 1995).

February 4, 1994, Dramaten, Stockholm
Feuer, chor. and perf., George Tabori, *Goldbergervariationer* (*Goldberg Variations*) (Ingmar Bergman, dir.)

April 29, 1994, Dramaten, Stockholm
Feuer, chor., Shakespeare, *Vintersagan* (*A Winter's Tale*) (Ingmar Bergman, dir.) (Almquist)
Performed at the Brooklyn Academy of Music, New York, May 31–June 3, 1995.

November 10, 1994, Sal Ett, Dramaten, Stockholm
Feuer, dir., Donya Feuer, *A Matter of the Heart*
Based on Ted Hughes's A Choice of Shakespeare's Verse.

1995, Kulturhuset, Stockholm
Feuer, dir., Shakespeare (Ted Hughes's version), *The Tempest*

1995, Sveriges Television, Stockholm
Feuer, dir., film *Martha Graham 100är: en hyllning dokumentär* (*Martha Graham's 100th Year: A Personal Birthday Greeting*)

February 17, 1995, Dramaten, Stockholm
Feuer, chor., Molière, *Misantropen* (*The Misanthrope*) (Ingmar Bergman, dir.)

May 14, 1995, Dramaten, Stockholm
Feuer, dir., *After Sibiu*
Based on Ted Hughes's A Choice of Shakespeare's Verse.

May 20, 1995, Merce Cunningham Studio, New York
Sanasardo (with John Passafiume), *The Seven Last Words* (Kancheli)
Sanasardo's tribute to Alum, and his last work to be seen in New York.

November 24, 1995, Dramaten, Stockholm
> Feuer, chor., Witold Gombrowicz, *Yvonne, princessa av Burgund* (*Yvonne, Princess of Burgundy*) (Ingmar Bergman, dir.)

1996, Stockholm
> Feuer receives the Carina Ari Gold Medal for her contribution to the art of dance in Sweden.

March 15, 1996, Dramaten, Stockholm
> Feuer, chor. and perf. (as Talata), Euripedes, *Backanterna* (*The Bacchae*) (Ingmar Bergman, dir.)

February 5, 1997, Norrlands Operan, Oslo
> Feuer, dir., Gian Carlo Menotti, *Mediet* (*The Medium*)
> Peter Weiss and Ulf Björlin, *Kasper Rosenröd*

1998, Stockholm
> Feuer receives Stockholm's Stads Heders Pris for her "groundbreaking" Shakespeare Project in cooperation with England's poet laureate Ted Hughes.

January 12, 1998, In the Company of Shakespeare, Dramaten, Stockholm
> Feuer, dir., *För "groundlings" och deras vänner* (*For Groundlings and Their Friends*)

1999, Sweden
> Feuer, dir., film *The Working of Utopia* (with Kevin Haigen and the Hamburg Ballet)

December 16, 2000, Dramaten, Stockholm
> Feuer, chor., Friedrich Schiller, *Maria Stuarda* (*Mary Stuart*) (Ingmar Bergman, dir.)
> *Performed at the Brooklyn Academy of Music, New York, June 12–16, 2002.*

December 13, 2002, Swedish Royal Opera, Stockholm
> Feuer, chor., *Nektergalen* (*The Nightingale*) (dir. Gunnel Lindblom) (Stravinsky)

Notes

Notes to Preface, pp. xvi–xxi

1. The books of Sally Banes have put Judson "on the map" to such an extent that the map has become somewhat unbalanced. See her *Terpsichore in Sneakers: Post-Modern Dance* (Middletown, Conn.: Wesleyan University Press, 1977) and *Democracy's Body: Judson Dance Theatre, 1962–1964* (Middletown, Conn.: Wesleyan University Press, 1993). Recently, Susan Leigh Foster's *Dances That Describe Themselves: The Improvised Choreography of Richard Bull* (Middletown, Conn.: Wesleyan University Press, 2002) has opened another area of dance started in the sixties to discussion.

2. The issue of the artist anecdote as both artist biography and critical commentary has been insightfully treated in Catherine Soussloff, *The Absolute Artist: The Historiography of a Concept* (Minneapolis: University of Minnesota Press, 1997), 145–158.

3. Richard Schechner and Willa Appel, "Introduction," *By Means of Performance: Intercultural Studies of Theatre and Ritual*, ed. Schechner and Appel (Cambridge: Cambridge University Press, 1990), 4.

4. José Gil, *Metamorphoses of the Body*, trans. Stephan Meucke (Minneapolis: University of Minnesota University Press, 1998), ix. Gilles Deleuze and Félix Guattari discuss intensities as "lines of flight" in *A Thousand Plateaus: Capitalism and Schizophrenia*, trans. Brian Massumi (Minneapolis: University of Minnesota Press, 1987).

5. Frank Stella, interview by Terry Gross, *Fresh Air*, NPR, November 16, 2000.

6. Paul Sanasardo, letter to the author, December 8, 1999. Most of the testimony I shall cite is from personal letters and taped interviews. I have decided not to encumber the text with documentation about every quotation unless it is has been published.

7. Sontag concludes, "In place of a hermeneutics we need an erotics of art." *Against Interpretation* (New York: Farrar, Straus and Giroux, 1966), 14.

8. Philip Auslander, *Presence and Resistance: Postmodernism and Cultural Politics in Contemporary American Performance* (Ann Arbor: University of Michigan Press, 1994), 37.

9. Sontag, *Against Interpretation*, 7.

10. Poststructuralists frequently appealed to the operations of theater, gesture, and space, for which conventional philosophical or humanistic discourse was perceived as inadequate.

Notes to Chapter One, pp. 1–31

1. I shall also briefly evoke certain individually authored works created both before and after the late fifties and early sixties.

2. The evening-length work familiar to nineteenth-century ballet was practically unknown in American modern dance. The only example of it concurrent with the work of Sanasardo and Feuer was Martha Graham's *Clytemnestra* (1958). Yvonne Rainer's evening-length *Terrain* premiered in 1963. The only remotely comparable choreographic use of children that I have seen is Tatsumi Hijikata's choreography for the film *War Games* (*Senso gokko*) (1960). For a comparison of Sanasardo and Feuer's use of children with that of Isadora Duncan, see p. 81.

3. Exception should be made for the phenomenon of dual authorship handed down in certain nineteenth-century romantic ballets where there was a division of choreographic labor. For example, one choreographer might set the large corps de ballet sequences, while another would be called in to choreograph for the soloists.

4. As of 1952 Feuer was an understudy and apprentice for roles in *Letter to the World, Deaths and Entrances,* and *Diversion of Angels.*

5. On the impact of *Rooms*, see Larry Warren, *Anna Sokolow: The Rebellious Spirit* (Princeton: Princeton Book Company, 1991), 148–155. *Rooms* premiered on February 24, 1955, at the 92nd Street Y.

6. *I'll Be You and You Be Me* premiered on a Dance Associates program at the Master Institute Theater on April 26, 1955. Feuer had already presented three short works—*With Love, Vigil,* and *Two Songs*—in a 1954 concert shared with Richard Englund and Linda Margolies at the Educational Alliance, 197 West Broadway, New York.

7. *Red Roses for Me* premiered on December 28, 1955, at the Booth Theater. The distinguished cast included Kevin McCarthy, Eileen Crowe, Joyce Sullivan, and E. G. Marshall. Graham's Asian tour lasted from October 1955 until February 1956. See Naima Prevots, *Dance for Export: Cultural Diplomacy and the Cold War* (Middletown, Conn.: Wesleyan University Press, 1998), 45–52.

8. The program consisted of the reprise of Feuer's *I'll Be You* and her *Chamber Music*—Sanasardo's *Three Dances of Death in the Grand Manner*, Widman's *Suite*, and Taylor's *Untitled Duet, Three Epitaphs*, and *The Least Flycatcher*.

9. The letter, sent to potential donors, is dated January 28, 1957. The performance took place on April 8, 1957, at the Rooftop Theatre at Second Avenue and Houston Street.

10. Each work was a trio: Feuer cast Sanasardo and Anneliese Widman, while Sanasardo cast Feuer and the poet Ellen Green, whom they had met at the Graham studio.

11. "Stephan Durkee, Robert Indiana, and Richard Smith (Dance Studio)," *Art News* 60, no. 4 (summer 1961): 16.

12. Jane Jacobs, *The Death and Life of Great American Cities* (New York: Random House, 1961), 257.

13. A sense of Chelsea's former glories is transmitted in Willa Cather's short story "Paul's Case: A Study in Temperament," in *The Troll Garden* (New York: New American Library, 1961), 117–138. Cather was one of Sanasardo's favorite authors.

14. Other dancers in the company of this period included Loretta Abbott, Art Bauman, Chifra Holt, Michelle and Millagro Llauger, Ellen Marshall, and Jack Weber.

15. Although Bausch's choreographic career officially begins with *Fragmente (Fragments)* in 1968, it might also be traced back to the collaborative *Phases of Madness* in 1960.

16. Bassoonist Arthur Weisberg, a champion of modern music, founded the Contemporary Chamber Ensemble in 1960. This tour was likely a warmup for the group's official debut on September 25, 1960, when they played Ives, Webern, Petrassi, Blackwood, and Schoenberg. They probably met Weisberg through Moshe Neuman, a musician who had performed in *I'll Be You and You Be Me* and who married Royal Ballet dancer Angela Walton. Walton was also to perform with Sanasardo and Feuer in the early sixties, taking on the Bausch role in *In View of God*.

17. For a discussion of the relation of madness to the development of theatrical dancing in the late nineteenth and early twentieth century, see Felicia McCarren, *Dance Pathologies: Performance, Poetics, Medicine* (Stanford: Stanford University Press, 1998).

18. Michel Foucault's research into madness, which questioned the distance of that malady from normality, was first published in France in 1961 as *Histoire de la folie à l'âge classique*. Sanasardo, Feuer, and Bausch worked on madness separately from but simultaneously with Foucault's research.

19. I return to the question of freedom and madness in *Laughter after All* in chapter 5.

20. The company was later incorporated as Modern Dance Artists, Inc. Studio for Dance remained the name of the school.

21. For the history of this important venue for modern dance, see Naomi M. Jackson, *Converging Movements: Modern Dance and Jewish Culture at the 92nd Street Y* (Middletown, Conn.: Wesleyan University Press, 2000).

22. Fredric Jameson has used the term "micro-groups" to characterize sixties social formations in "Periodizing the Sixties," in *The Sixties without Apology,* ed. Sohnya Sayres et al. (Minneapolis: University of Minnesota Press, 1984), 187.

23. Alum's first work was shown in a shared concert with Judith Blackstone and Diane Germaine at Judson Hall in New York City on October 5, 1963, under the sponsorship of Studio for Dance. Later, he choreographed and taught internationally, but his own company also existed in symbiosis with Sanasardo's: he left without leaving. He was a riveting soloist whose intensity had a cool, almost schizoid detachment. His work was generally more spare than that of Sanasardo-Feuer. Among Alum's notable accomplishments was his invention of the danced travelogue for soloist with *Made in Japan* (1979) and for intercultural cast with *Made in Malaysia: A Shamanic Journey* (1991). Alum initiated a form of choreographic multiculturalism in the late seventies, and his work deserves more attention than is possible here.

24. Feuer trained Mats Ek and Niklas Ek, who debuted in 1963 in her ballets *Ekon* (*Echo*) and *Angels by Chance.*

25. The review by Walter Sorell, however, was quite positive overall. "Paul Sanasardo, Donya Feuer and Company," *Dance Observer* 30, no. 3 (March 1963): 40.

26. This is especially evident in her dance films for Norwegian television of the early seventies: *Frukost* (*The Breakfast*) and *Et syn* (*A Way of Seeing*). In both films, dancers both play and dance roles without text. Other films Feuer shot for television include *With the Body as Downpayment* and *Life Is the Time It Takes Me to Die.*

27. A film shot during this period of the company's history, *Cyclometry* (1971), shows performances at the Schenectady Museum, New York, and was broadcast frequently on public television during the seventies.

28. Alum also played in Feuer's short pilot film *Taxinge-Näsby Station* (1972) and performed the role originally created for Jens Graff in *God Is Alive and Well* at the Royal Dramatic Theater.

29. Sanasardo created *Saints and Lovers* for the Ballet Théâtre Contemporain in Angers, France, and five works for Bat-Dor Dance Company in Tel Aviv between 1971 and 1975. The Sanasardo Company was always based in New York and toured the United States from coast to coast (as well as

Bermuda, Nassau, and Puerto Rico) between 1963 and 1976. It never undertook a foreign tour, but Sanasardo's foreign commissions weakened his tie to the company over time.

30. The artists' having worked in so many foreign countries raises the complex issues of dance in relation to national identity. How can Bausch's influences be evenly split between Sanasardo-Feuer and the older Freie Tanz of Mary Wigman when Sanasardo himself is also linked to the German tradition through Strongstoff and Thimey? And can the socially conscious tradition of the American Left (Sokolow and Chilkovsky) as filtered through Sanasardo-Feuer also be recognized in Bausch?

31. Although he disbanded his company in 1986, the last of Sanasardo's work to be seen in New York, choreographed in collaboration with John Passafiume, was his homage to Alum, who died of AIDS on May 11, 1993: *The Seven Last Words* was performed at the Merce Cunningham Studio in May 1994.

32. See Mark Franko, *The Work of Dance: Movement, Labor, and Identity in the 1930s* (Middletown, Conn.: Wesleyan University Press, 2002).

33. Chilkovsky herself performed Isadora Duncan's choreography during the 1920s with Irma Duncan. In the 1930s she danced with Hanya Holm and worked on the Federal Dance Project as dancer and choreographer. In the 1940s, after trying to invent her own dance notation system, she took private lessons in Labanotation with Anne Hutchinson at the Dance Notation Bureau in New York. Nadia Chilkovsky, telephone interview with author, September 15, 2001.

34. Sanasardo discusses his Italian background in the film *American Stories*.

35. Thimey, a student of Mary Wigman, immigrated to Chicago in 1932. She performed in the United States with the expatriate German Jewish dancer Jan Veen (a.k.a. Hans Wiener).

36. Marcuse defines affirmative culture as "the assertion of a universally obligatory, eternally better and more valuable world that must be unconditionally affirmed: a world different from the factual world of the daily struggle for existence, yet realizable by every individual 'from within', without any transformation of the state of fact." See Herbert Marcuse, *Negations: Essays in Critical Theory* (London: Free Association Books, 1988), 95. In my analyses of *Excursion for Miracles* and *Laughter after All* I draw on the critical context of German Marxism in the 1920s (Lukács) and its American transposition in the sixties (Marcuse).

37. Judith Chazin-Bennahum, *The Ballets of Antony Tudor: Studies in Psyche and Satire* (New York: Oxford University Press, 1994), 189.

38. Sanasardo, however, like Paul Taylor, felt the need to emancipate

himself from Graham's influence in the fifties. For example, he was not entirely happy with *Of Human Kindness* because the set he designed, once it was on the stage, reminded him of Isamu Noguchi's set for Graham's *Canticle for Innocent Comedians.*

39. Slavenska was a member of the Ballets Russes de Monte Carlo before coming to the United States. Feuer remembers that she was the only teacher in New York at that time to hold professional class on Sundays, thus setting the example of studying seven days a week.

40. Sara Rudner, interview by Rose Ann Thom, 1995, interview 24, transcript, Dance History Project, Dance Collection, New York Public Library.

41. Perhaps for this reason, ballet dancers such as Lawrence Rhodes and Naomi Sorkin were also drawn to work with Sanasardo in the seventies. He created *Andantino Cantabile* for them in 1976, and Sorkin appeared as a guest with the company in other works.

42. This phrase is from the film's promotional copy.

43. These films are perhaps the first attempt to deal with Nijinsky not in terms of his fame, but in terms of his madness. They also represent an attempt to correlate his madness directly to his artistic vision and his relationship to the public.

44. Through her production work at Statens Musikdramatiska Skola (State Opera School) Feuer brought new approaches to the staging of historical opera (Gluck, Händel, and Mozart) and influenced the style of opera staging in Sweden.

45. Although Feuer choreographed Bergman's film *The Magic Flute* (1973), her collaboration with Bergman has been predominantly in the medium of live theater.

46. Paul Sanasardo, interview by John Gruen, March 26, 1975, in preparation for an article in *Dance Magazine*. The audiotape is archived in the Dance Collection, Lincoln Center Library for the Performing Arts. In their own choreography, both Sokolow and Lang used Sanasardo to dramatic rather than lyrical effect.

47. Jacques Baril, *La Danse moderne d'Isadora Duncan à Twyla Tharp* (Paris: Editions Vigot, 1977), 346 (my translation).

48. This analysis was made in reference to Shirley Clarke's film *A Moment in Love* (1957) with Sanasardo and Carmela Gutierrez. It serves to document Sanasardo's performance qualities in the fifties. Sokolow adapted her choreography for this film from several previously choreographed duets.

49. Judith Blackstone, *The Subtle Self: Personal Growth and Spiritual Practice* (Berkeley: North Atlantic Books, 1991), 1.

50. Lilith, Adam's first wife, was a Jewish female demon and symbol of

sensual lust. Art Bauman, interview by Lesley Farlow, 1992, transcript, Oral History Project of the Dance Collection, Lincoln Center Library for the Performing Arts, New York, 40.

51. David Shapiro, "Art as Collaboration: Toward a Theory of Pluralist Aesthetics, 1950–1980," in *Artistic Collaboration in the Twentieth Century*, ed. Cynthia Jaffee McCabe (Washington, D.C.: Smithsonian Institution Press, 1984), 45.

52. Paul Sanasardo, interview by John Gruen for "The Sound of Dance," WNCN-FM, New York, broadcast June 12, 1977. A sound recording is archived in the Dance Collection, New York Public Library for the Performing Arts.

53. Comments drawn from a filmed interview about Feuer's *The Working of Utopia*, recorded in English in Sweden. Film in author's personal collection.

54. Glenn Meredith Loney, "'I Pick My Dancers as People': Pina Bausch Discusses Her Work with the Wuppertal Dance Theatre," *On the Next Wave: Brooklyn Academy of Music Special Dance Issue* 3, nos. 1–2 (October 1985), 14.

55. Sanasardo here borrows Graham's language: "I am a thief—but with this reservation—I think I know the value of that I steal and I treasure it for all time." Martha Graham quoted by Nancy Wilson Ross, "Introduction," *The Notebooks of Martha Graham* (New York: Harcourt Brace Jovanovich, 1973), 6.

56. Sally Banes uses the term "confusion of frames" with reference to Jack Gelber's *The Connection*. See Sally Banes, *Greenwich Village, 1963: Avant-Garde Performance and the Effervescent Body* (Durham, N.C.: Duke University Press, 1993), 117. On the concept of nonmatrixed theater, see Michael Kirby, *Happenings: An Illustrated Anthology* (New York: E. P. Dutton, 1965), 16–17.

57. Kirby, *Happenings*, 16.

58. The dual rejection of inside/outside and narrative in poststructuralist thought entails the structural disadvantage of equating depth and linearity in a single figure. This is one reason why this critique is not supple enough for Sanasardo and Feuer or Bausch.

59. There are doubtless family connections between this and what Norbert Servos calls, apropos of Pina Bausch's work, "a theatre of experience." See Norbert Servos, *Pina Bausch-Wuppertal Dance Theater, or, The Art of Training a Goldfish: Excursions into Dance*, trans. Patricia Stadié (Cologne: Ballett-Bühnen-Verlag, 1984), 37. Bausch also manipulates role playing as a way of putting identities into question.

Notes to Chapter Two, pp. 33–68

1. The effect here is to place performance outside its traditional (representational) theatrical sphere, since what the curtain opens onto is what we already know or have just seen. But this move is as much toward surrealism as toward realism, since what we have seen and will see is just as likely to be on the far side of implausibility.

2. See Peter Fuller, *Robert Natkin* (New York: Harry N. Abrams, 1981).

3. Due to an injury, Germaine did not actually perform in the 1964 version. Replacing her, Loretta Abbott played both a Woman in High Heels and One Woman.

4. G. W. F. Hegel, *The Phenomenology of Mind* (New York: Harper and Row, 1967), 93–94.

5. "Although melancholy always contains the moment of nostalgia, nostalgia is not necessarily melancholic. Nostalgia is often the ideological and feeling aspect of a new choice of values and tasks." Agnes Heller, *A Theory of Feelings* (Assen, Netherlands: Van Gorcum, 1979), 187.

Notes to Chapter Three, pp. 49–87

1. Blackstone's family name was Bloodstein. Sanasardo and Feuer thought of Eva Carlotta as a stage name for Judith. Feuer's second choice was Bloodstone. Judith later decided on Blackstone, taking the word "black" from Schwarz, her mother's maiden name.

2. The costumes were designed and executed by Martha Graham's seamstress Ursula Reed.

3. Lillian Moore, "Review," *Dance Magazine* 32, no. 4 (April 1958), 80.

4. Judith Blackstone, *The Subtle Self: Personal Growth and Spiritual Practice* (Berkeley: North Atlantic Books, 1991), 2.

5. Rainer Maria Rilke, *Letters to a Young Poet*, trans. M. D. Herter Norton (New York: Norton, 1934), 17.

6. Rainer Maria Rilke, *Selected Works: Prose*, trans. G. Craig Houston (London: Hogarth, 1961), 1:145.

7. "Wir kennen den Kontur des Fühlens nicht, nur was ihn formt von aussen." Rainer Maria Rilke, *Duino Elegies*, trans. J. B. Leishman and Stephen Spender (New York: Norton, 1939), 40–41. (I have slightly modified the translation to conform closely to the original.) Feuer would later work directly with *Duino Elegies* in her *Ej blot til lyst* (1985).

8. Feuer was then reading Ernest Fenollosa and Ezra Pound's *The Classic Noh Theatre of Japan* (1917; Westport, Conn.: Greenwood Press, 1977).

9. The children included Judith Blackstone, Kathlyn Bushnell, Tamara Drasin, Elaine Fischman, Willa Kahn, Randi Rubin, Wendy Wolosoff, Judy Canner, Daniel Canner, Jo-Ellen Epstein, Ruth Frank, Nina Lehrman, and Susan Underwood.

10. Feuer's role is truer to Rilke's poetic insight: "But because being here amounts to so much, because all this Here and Now, so fleeting, seems to require us and strongly concerns us. Us the most fleeting of all." Rilke, *Duino Elegies*, 73.

11. Walter Sorell, "Review," *Dance Magazine* 33, no. 6 (June 1959), 92.

12. Sorell, "Review," 92.

13. Selma-Jeanne Cohen, "Review," *Dance Magazine* 35, no. 1 (January 1961), 61.

14. "Each torpid turn of the world," writes Rilke in the *Duino Elegies*, "has such disinherited children, to whom no longer what's been, and not yet what's coming, belong" (63).

15. "O Stunden in der Kindheit, da hinter den Figuren mehr als nur Vergangnes war und vor uns nicht die Zukunft." Rilke, *Duino Elegies*, 45.

16. "Im Zwischenraume zwischen Welt und Spielzeug." Rilke, *Duino Elegies*, 44. Feuer returned to this text in 1975 with *Ej blot til lyst* (*Not Just as an Amusement*).

17. "An einer Stelle, die seit Anbeginn gegründet war für einen reinen Vorgang." Rilke, *Duino Elegies*, 44.

18. The event is synonymous with the figure for Lyotard as "a discharge (*décharge*) coming from an other order" ("Elle est un effet de décharge provenant d'un autre ordre"). Jean-François Lyotard, *Discours, figure* (Paris: Klincksieck, 1971), 146.

19. Other images remain too faded for interpretation: the children covered in opaque white glass chains, the presence of a skull (designed by graphic artist Dick Tyler, who also designed the poster).

20. "Wer zeigt ein Kind, so wie es steht?" Rilke, *Duino Elegies*, 44.

21. Cohen, "Review," 61.

22. Sorell, "Review," 92.

23. *I'll Be You and You Be Me* was performed twice in 1955 before Feuer's departure to Asia, and again in 1956.

24. The text was adapted from Ruth Krauss's *I'll Be You and You Be Me*, illustrated by Maurice Sendak (New York: Harper and Row, 1954). Ellen Green appeared in their other text-based productions of this period, such as Feuer's *A Serious Dance for Three Fools* (based on Virginia Woolf's *The Waves*) and Sanasardo's *Doctor Faustus Lights the Lights* (based on the Gertrude Stein play); both premiered in 1957. Green was a British poet whom Martha Graham had admitted into her professional class.

25. Krauss, *I'll Be You and You Be Me*.

26. *Three Dances of Death* premiered on June 5, 1956, on a Dance Associates program at the Master Institute, which was curated by James Waring. Also on the program was Feuer's *I'll Be You and You Be Me* and *Chamber*

Music, Anneliese Widman's *Suite,* and Paul Taylor's *Untitled Duet, Three Epitaphs,* and *The Least Flycatcher.*

27. Michel Foucault, *The Birth of the Clinic: An Archaeology of Medical Perception,* trans. R. M. Sheridan Smith (New York: Vintage Books, 1994), 171. Foucault links tuberculosis and passion in the passage on the basis of this singular identity that they achieve in and by death. He concludes that "Death . . . became the lyrical core of man" (172).

28. Feuer's solo *Självporträtt I: ragtime för en princessa* (*Selfportrait I: Ragtime for a Princess*) (1964), inspired by Edward Steichen's portrait of Princess Yousupov, also references her role as Aunt Tina in *Pictures in Our House.* But this lightheartedness combined with nostalgia was unusual in the further work of both artists.

29. This paragraph is taken from a conversation between Paul Sanasardo and John Gruen, 1977.

30. "Riter bakom de borgerliga fasademrna." Alf Sjöberg, notes for his production of *The Fire and the Water,* quoted in Feuer's program for her production of Strindberg's *Easter* (1981).

Notes to Chapter Four, pp. 89–120

1. David Riesman, Nathan Glazer, and Reuel Denney, *The Lonely Crowd: A Study of the Changing American Character* (New Haven: Yale University Press, 1950), xxvii.

2. Reisman et al., *The Lonely Crowd,* 274–275.

3. Sanasardo was also influenced in Chicago by Bruno Bettelheim. He was introduced to psychoanalytic circles in Chicago through his friend Florence Hamlish Levinsohn, who later wrote books on politics and urban affairs.

4. Herbert Marcuse, *Eros and Civilization: A Philosophical Inquiry into Freud* (Boston: Beacon, 1966), 96.

5. William H. Whyte Jr., *The Organization Man* (New York: Simon and Schuster, 1956), 12 (my emphasis).

6. Paul Goodman, *Growing Up Absurd* (New York: Vintage Books, 1960), 14. Although Riesman briefly discussed sex as a road toward autonomy, he omitted homosexuality, whereas Goodman did not.

7. See Paul Goodman, *Five Years* (New York: Brussel and Brussel, 1966).

8. "Here the notion 'aesthetic' is taken in its original sense, namely as the form of sensitivity of the senses and as the form of the concrete world of human life." Herbert Marcuse, *Five Lectures—Psychoanalysis, Politics, Utopia* (Boston: Beacon, 1970), 68. Inasmuch as the aesthetic dimension calls on real life as an arena for gratification, it implicitly refers us to the everyday. Charles Reitz locates the important critical moments in Marcuse's thought

as 1937, 1955, and 1964 in his *Art, Alienation, and the Humanities: A Critical Engagement with Herbert Marcuse* (Albany: State University of New York Press, 2000).

9. The operative concept of everyday behavior as performance derives from the managerial business context. See Erving Goffman, *The Presentation of Self in Everyday Life* (New York: Doubleday, 1959).

10. Herbert Marcuse, *One-Dimensional Man: Studies in the Ideology of Advanced Industrial Society* (Boston: Beacon, 1964), 124.

11. Marcuse, *One-Dimensional Man*, 158. Marcuse's work in and about the sixties was grounded in his personal familiarity with and critical treatment of Fascism in Europe during the 1930s. It was thus, despite its popularity, more than a pop phenomenon: it was grounded in a complex historical dimension. See Herbert Marcuse, *Collected Papers of Herbert Marcuse*, vol. 1, *Technology, War and Fascism*, ed. Douglas Kellner (London: Routledge, 1998).

12. For a discussion of the ambiguity in the concept of the everyday as typified in the work of Henri Lefebvre, see Anselm Jappe, *Guy Debord* (Berkeley and Los Angeles: University of California Press, 1999), 76–80.

13. Louis Horst, "Review," *Dance Observer* 24, no. 9 (November 1957), 139.

14. Jill Johnston sees this review as an honest piece of performative criticism. See "Critic's Critics," in *Marmalade Me* (New York: Dutton, 1971), 100–102. The counterpart to Horst's reaction might be found in the hysterical review of Walter Terry, who accused Taylor of trying to "drive his captive audience insane." Walter Terry, "Experiment? Joke? Or War of Nerves?" *New York Herald Tribune*, October 27, 1957, sec. 4, 6.

15. Doris Hering, "Review," *Dance Magazine* 31, no. 22 (December 1957), 83–84.

16. Francis Sparshott's 1988 discussion of *Seven New Dances* also focuses on the issues of stillness. Sparshott challenged critics to engage with the work in its full context, yet he limited what context means to the work's formal attributes. See his *Off the Ground: First Steps to a Philosophical Consideration of Dance* (Princeton: Princeton University Press, 1988), 245–249. I agree with Sparshott that *Seven New Dances* needs to be considered in its entirety, something I cannot do here. But I would add that the entirety of the work also includes what lies outside the work's formal confines. On this theoretical point, see my "Dance and Figurability," in *The Salt of the Earth: On Dance, Politics, and Reality*, ed. Steven de Belder (Brussels: Flemish Theater Institute, 2001), 33–57.

17. Lincoln Kirstein, "The Monstrous Itch," *New York Review of Books* 34, no. 10 (June 11, 1987), 30–32.

18. Kirstein, "The Monstrous Itch," 30.

19. "David Tudor comes to the piano and just sits for four minutes and

thirty-three seconds, silently deploying his arms three times in ways that suggest the work might have three distinct movements." Richard Kostelanetz, "Inferential Art," in *John Cage* (New York: Praeger, 1970), 107. Tudor performed *4'33"* in *Resemblance,* the third dance of *Seven New Dances.*

20. The notoriety that *Seven New Dances* achieved has been credited for launching Taylor's choreographic career. "Relatively few people had attended the concert," writes Angela Kane, "but Louis Horst's non-review . . . was largely responsible for Taylor's first taste of fame." Angela Kane, "Paul Taylor," in *International Encyclopedia of Dance* (New York: Oxford University Press, 1988), 6:108.

21. Paul Taylor, *Private Domain* (New York: Knopf, 1987), 76.

22. Taylor, *Private Domain,* 77.

23. Taylor, *Private Domain,* 77. Taylor expatiates on this: "The natural movements, when done in a dancy way, look unnatural, and so we have to find a new, yet equally stylized, way to do them. We memorize vast amounts of uneven counts in order to give rhythmic variety and to keep from falling into monotony."

24. All the quotations in this paragraph are from Taylor, *Private Domain,* 78.

25. Taylor, *Private Domain,* 77. Hering noted that the "dancers seemed subtly alive and concentrated" despite their immobility. Hering, "Review," 84.

26. Marcuse, *One-Dimensional Man,* 10.

27. Marcuse, *One-Dimensional Man,* 23.

28. The connection between Taylor's choreographic reduction and de Certeau's tactics, or "productive consumption," cannot be developed here. On the difference between tactics and strategy, see Michel de Certeau, *The Practice of Everyday Life,* trans. Steven Rendall (Berkeley and Los Angeles: University of California Press, 1984), xviii–xx. See also Gianni Vattimo's comments on the death of art in advanced technological society in *The End of Modernity. Nihilism and Hermeneutics in Postmodern Culture,* trans. Jon R. Snyder (Baltimore: Johns Hopkins University Press, 1985), 51 sq.

29. See Jürgen Habermas, *The Structural Transformation of the Public Sphere: An Inquiry into a Category of Bourgeois Society,* trans. Thomas Burger with Frederick Lawrence (Cambridge, Mass: MIT Press, 1994), 48–49.

30. Marcuse, *One-Dimensional Man,* 13.

31. Paul Sanasardo, letter to author, October 1, 1999. "I am not sure how the work was received," he added, "although the better part of the audience did return for the second night."

32. Marcuse, *Eros and Civilization,* 194.

33. Henry M. Sayre relates drifting to Deleuzian intensity. He cites "a

sense that the work is being driven by forces other than the author, that it is informed, as it were, by chance collisions and whatever occurs at its margins." See Sayre, *The Object of Performance: The American Avant-Garde since 1970* (Chicago: University of Chicago Press, 1989), 147.

34. In terms of method, it suggests a structural analogy with Taylor's approach to found positions. As Feuer has remarked, "The program was like having the positions and finding the movement that would take you there." Here, the positionality was less performative and more choreographic. The program was like Taylor's charts in that it mapped certain possibilities.

35. Walter Terry, "Sanasardo-Feuer," in *New York Herald Tribune*, December 16, 1961.

36. Marcia Marks, "Review," *Dance Magazine* 35, no. 12 (December 1961), 37.

37. Terry, "Sanasardo-Feuer."

38. Lyda Borelli was the first silent film star of Italian cinema, appearing in eleven films between 1913 and 1918. In 1917 Antonio Grasci called her "a piece of prehistoric primordial humanity" ("un pezzo di umanità prehistorica, primordiale"). Gramsci, quoted in *Star al femminile*, ed. Gian Luca Farinelli and Jean-Loup Passek (Ancona: Transeuropa, 2000), 58. I thank Eugenia Casini-Ropa for calling my attention to this book, and Helena Robinson for research on Borelli's filmography.

39. Marks, "Review," 60.

40. Marks, "Review," 60.

41. Marks, "Review," 60.

42. Marks seems to refer to the Borelli figure and so may have mistaken Llauger for Feuer. The first version of Graham's *Cave of the Heart* was titled *The Serpent's Tail*.

43. Charles Reitz, *Art, Alienation, and the Humanities: A Critical Engagement with Herbert Marcuse* (Albany: State University of New York Press, 2000), 144. "Sex," notes Marcuse, "is integrated into work and public relations and is thus made more susceptible to (controlled) satisfaction." This "scientific management of the libido" leads to a "de-erotization of the environment." Marcuse, *One-Dimensional Man*, 75. As Riesman observed of other-directed culture: "Escape diminishes by the very fact that work and pleasure are interlaced." *The Lonely Crowd*, 141.

44. See Sally Banes, *Greenwich Village 1963: Avant-Garde Performance and the Effervescent Body* (Durham, N.C.: Duke University Press, 1993).

45. Marcuse, *One-Dimensional Man*, 33.

46. Marcuse, *One-Dimensional Man*, 188.

47. Marcuse, *One-Dimensional Man*, 10.

48. Marcuse, *One-Dimensional Man*, 132.

49. Marcuse, *One-Dimensional Man,* 87.

50. Maurice Blanchot, *The Writing of the Disaster,* trans. Ann Smock (Lincoln: University of Nebraska Press, 1986), 3.

51. *Metallics* was first performed by Elina Mooney, Willa Kahn, and Manuel Alum for the company's midwestern tour in 1963. It has been taken into the repertory of the Alvin Ailey Dance Company, the First Chamber Dance Quartet, the Netherlands Dance Theatre, Bat Dor, and the Winnipeg Repertory Company.

52. Henri Lefebvre, *Critique of Everyday Life,* trans. John Moore (London: Verso, 2000), 32.

Notes to Chapter Five, pp. 121–142

1. *Laughter after All* premiered on June 18, 1960, and was performed again on December 4, 1960, and in a "revised" version on February 1, 1964, at Hunter Playhouse in New York City. Sounds were taped and arranged by Jan Syrjala. The music was by Edgard Varèse (*Density 21.5, Ionization, Octandre, Integrales,* and *Poème Electronique*). Varèse also provided further taped sounds. Robert Natkin designed the set and costumes, and Nicola Cernovich designed the lighting.

2. What follows is a brief résumé of Lukács's philosophical argument in Georg Lukács, "Reification and the Consciousness of the Proletariat," in *History and Class Consciousness: Studies in Marxist Dialectics,* trans. Rodney Livingstone (Cambridge, Mass.: MIT Press, 1971). See also Eugene Lunn, *Marxism and Modernism: An Historical Study of Lukács, Brecht, Benjamin and Adorno* (Berkeley and Los Angeles: University of California Press, 1982), 97–98.

3. Or, as Raymond Williams puts it, "All 'objects,' and in this context notably works of art, are *mediated* by specific social relations but cannot be reduced to an abstraction of that relationship." *Keywords: A Vocabulary of Culture and Society* (New York: Oxford University Press, 1983), 206.

4. Conversely, mimetic strategies that pertain to "distortion" and are "inherently physical" can, as in Susan Kozel's understanding of Pina Bausch, "transform the associated social and aesthetic space." See Susan Kozel, "'The Story Is Told as a History of the Body': Strategies of Mimesis in the Work of Irigaray and Bausch," in *Meaning in Motion: New Cultural Studies of Dance,* ed. Jane C. Desmond (Durham, N.C.: Duke University Press, 1997), 101. Bausch continues the Sanasardo-Feuer interest in pathological behaviors as forms of mimetic distortion.

5. R. C. Allen, *Horrible Prettiness: Burlesque and American Culture* (Chapel Hill: University of North Carolina Press, 1991), 129. Allen's study points to the difficulties of interpreting the historical burlesque, citing a contempo-

rary report that "though they were not like men, [they] were in most things as unlike women, and seemed creatures of a kind of alien sex, parodying both. It was certainly a shocking thing to look at them with their horrible prettiness, their archness in which was no charm, their grace which put to shame" (134–135). The menacing demeanor of the Five Women in High Heels contradicts their more modern reference to a burlesque sexuality and brings *Laughter* in line with burlesque's historical complexity. Allen's position is that burlesque performance was initially erotic, amusing, and disturbing, but he is unable to specify the concerns of its transgressiveness.

6. Karl Marx, *Capital*, trans. Samuel Moore and Edward Aveling (New York: International Publishers, 1984), 1:44. Exchange value induces us to evaluate everything in relation to a market. The market, by definition, has isolated things from their sources and abstracted them from their destinations. As commodities, things are fetishistic, that is, fascinating in their insular and autonomous appeal to our needs. Use value, on the other hand, refers to things only inasmuch as they intrinsically address and satisfy our needs as well as reflect our subjectivity and the subject positions in which our needs originate. This is what Baudrillard refers to as the theocracy of use value: "But value in the case of use value is enveloped in total mystery, for it is grounded anthropologically in the (self-) 'evidence' of a naturalness, in an unsurpassable original reference." Jean Baudrillard, *For a Critique of the Political Economy of the Sign*, trans. Charles Levin (St. Louis: Telos, 1981), 139.

7. Allen, *Horrible Prettiness*, 134 and 107.

8. Stuart Hall, "The Problem of Ideology—Marxism without Guarantees," *Journal of Communication Inquiry* 10.2 (1986), 35.

9. The ethos of the Women in High Heels is perhaps best summed up in the commentary of an informant described as "Patty, manager, former stripper" on the striptease performers whom Susan Meiselas photographed in small-town carnivals: "The girls aren't whores, they're not hustlers. They're working women. They're women with a job. . . . If you want to be your own woman, to be a single person, you can't do a hell of a lot better than that. Our only security is within ourselves and what we are able to do. That's all we really have. We can't depend on anybody loving us." Susan Meiselas, *Carnival Stripper* (New York: Farrar, Straus, and Giroux, 1976), 135–136.

10. This was not unheard of, however, in German modern dance. See, in particular, Valeska Gert's choreography in the 1920s and early 1930s, or more recently the work of Pina Bausch.

11. Lukács, "Reification and the Consciousness of the Proletariat," 166.

12. Christine Buci-Glucksmann, *La raison baroque: De Baudelaire à Benjamin* (Paris: Galilée, 1984), 120.

13. Allen, *Horrible Prettiness*, 198.

14. Sally Banes has remarked, "Like the Soviet avant-garde of the 1920s, the early Sixties artists were both interested in and historically capable of truly acknowledging the sophisticated mass culture they were part of—and the fact that they were part of it. They used computers and television, collaborated with engineers, and brought mass media techniques into the art gallery." *Greenwich Village 1963: Avant-Garde Performance and the Effervescent Body* (Durham, N.C.: Duke University Press, 1993), 7.

15. Jacqueline Maskey, "Review," *Dance Magazine* (March 1964), 64.

16. Herbert Marcuse, "The Affirmative Character of Culture," *Negations. Essays in Critical Theory* (London: Free Association Books, 1988), 129.

17. Karl Marx, *Grundrisse, Foundations of the Critique of Political Economy* (New York: Vintage, 1973), 93.

18. Allen, *Horrible Prettiness*, 134.

19. Allen, *Horrible Prettiness*, 283.

20. See Mark Franko, *Dancing Modernism/Performing Politics* (Bloomington: Indiana University Press, 1995).

21. "Rire est le propre de l'homme" ("laughter is man's most distinguishing feature"). Rabelais, *Oeuvres complètes* (Paris: Gallimard, 1955), 2.

22. As Blanchot put it, "Intensity cannot be called high or low without reestablishing the scale of values and principles characteristic of moderation's mediocre morality. Be it exertion or inertia, intensity is the extreme difference, in excess of the being that ontology takes for granted. Intensity is an excess, an absolute disruption which admits of no regimen, region, regulation, direction, erection, insur-rection, nor does it admit of their simplest contraries. . . . Whence the necessity to say that only exteriority, in its absolute separation, its infinite disintensification, returns to intensity the disastrous attractiveness that keeps it from being translated into revelation." *The Writing of the Disaster*, 56–57.

23. Gilles Deleuze, "Nomad Thought," in *The New Nietzsche*, ed. David B. Allison (Cambridge, Mass.: MIT Press, 1977), 146. Deleuze adds, "Intensity can be experienced then, only in connection with its mobile inscription of a body and under the shifting exterior of a proper name" (146–147). This explains the uncertain relation of dance to mimeticism or narrative.

24. "It is not true the search for intensities or things of that type can ground politics." Jean-François Lyotard and Jean-Loup Thébaud, *Just Gaming*, trans. Wald Godzich (Minneapolis: University of Minnesota Press, 1985), 90.

About the Author and Contributors

Mark Franko is a dancer, choreographer, and professor of dance and performance studies at the University of California in Santa Cruz. He has presented his choreography in the United States and Europe since 1985. His publications include *The Work of Dance* (Wesleyan University Press, 2002), *Dancing Modernism/Performing Politics* (1995), *Dance as Text: Ideologies of the Baroque Body* (1993), *The Dancing Body in Renaissance Choreography* (1986), and *Acting on the Past: Historical Performance across Disciplines* (coedited with Annette Richards, Wesleyan University Press, 2000). Franko was awarded a Getty fellowship and received research grants from the American Philosophical Society, the American Council of Learned Societies, and the France/Berkeley Fund. Among his numerous other awards are a Whiting fellowship and the 1966 De La Torre Bueno Award "Special Citation" for the best book in the field of dance for his book *Dancing Modernism/Performing Politics*. He holds an MA, an MPhil, and a PhD in French and Romance philology from Columbia University. His BA is from City College of New York.

Regina Axelrod danced with the Paul Sanasardo Dance Company in the 1960s and 1980s. With her partner, Garth Fagan, she started the Dance Theater of Detroit in 1966. She is now professor and chair of the Political Science Department at Adelphi University and has published books and articles on energy and environmental policy in the United States, the European Union, and Central and Eastern Europe.

Lynn (Scandur) Barr received her first training and professional experience with Paul Sanasardo and Donya Feuer. She went on to dance with the Philadelphia Lyric Opera and the New York City Opera and later formed her own company. In 1980 she returned to dance with Paul again. She continues to dance, teach, and choreograph in the United States, Italy, Poland, Germany, and most recently in Prague.

Pina Bausch worked with Paul Sanasardo and Donya Feuer from 1959 to 1960. In 1973 she founded the Wuppertaler Tanztheater, which has become one of the world's leading dance companies. Since then, her innovative choreography has been in the vanguard of European dance.

Judith Blackstone danced with the Paul Sanasardo Dance Company from 1957 to 1972. She is currently a psychotherapist and founder of Subtle Self Work: a method of integrating psychotherapy, spiritual attunement, and embodiment. She is author of *The Subtle Self, The Enlightenment Process,* and *Living Intimately,* and director of the Realization Center in Woodstock, New York.

Tamara Drasin was born and raised in Brooklyn, New York. She was invited to join a children's dance company run by Paul Sanasardo and Donya Feuer, participating from ages seven to thirteen. She now resides on Long Island with her family.

Diane Germaine was a leading dancer with the company from 1963 until 1976. She choreographed twenty-five works for Diane Germaine & Dancers and set works on Bat-Dor, Batsheva, the Kibbutz Dance Company, the Norsk Opera Ballett, and the London Contemporary Dance Theatre. She is currently based in Cincinnati, Ohio, where she choreographs and writes.

Chifra Holt was a soloist with Sanasardo and Feuer from 1959 until 1961 and also worked with Martha Graham, Alwin Nikolais, Robert Joffrey, and Benjamin Harkavy. She was associate professor and chair of dance at Wichita State University and currently resides in southern California.

Willa Kahn danced with Sanasardo and Feuer from 1959 to 1974 and also danced for Manuel Alum and Lar Lubovitch. She taught at Circle-in-the-Square Theatre School from 1972 to 1982. She is now a family physician at Great Brook Valley Health Center, Worcester, Massachusetts.

Joan Lombardi, a graduate of Parsons School of Design, danced with the Paul Sanasardo Dance Company from 1965 until 1984. She founded the Nova Arts Foundation, where she served as artistic director, choreographer, and performer. She is presently a full-time associate professor in the BFA Communication Design Department at the Fashion Institute of Technology of the State University of New York.

Ellen Marshall danced with Sanasardo and Feuer in the late fifties and early sixties. Following that, she performed and toured with Erick Hawkins, also teaching at his school. After living and teaching in upstate New York and Amsterdam, she returned to New York City to dance with Nancy Meehan and teach for her. She currently lives in New York City, where she is a massage therapist praticing and teaching tai chi chuan and qujong. She also dances and improvises with the group Old Enough To Know Better.

Judith (Canner) Moss began her professional career performing as a child with the Paul Sanasardo–Donya Feuer Children's Company, later joining the Paul Sanasardo Dance Company while in high school. After graduating from the University of Wisconsin, Moss danced for seven years with Dan Wagoner and Dancers. Having created over fifty dances for Judith Moss and Dancers, she currently teaches and conducts residencies at colleges and private studios throughout the United States and Europe.

Dominique Petit danced with the Paul Sanasardo Dance Company between 1969 and 1973. On his return to France he worked in Paris with Carolyn Carlson and produced his own work nationally and internationally. He currently teaches dance in Nantes, France.

Index

Library of Congress Cataloging-in-Publication Data

Franko, Mark.
Excursion for miracles : Paul Sanasardo, Donya
Feuer, and Studio for Dance, 1955–1964 / Mark
Franko.
     p. cm.
Includes index.
ISBN 0-8195-6743-4 (cloth : alk. paper)—
ISBN 0-8195-6744-2 (pbk. : alk. paper)
1. Feuer, Donya. 2. Sanasardo, Paul, 1928–
3. Choreographers—United States—Biography.
4. Studio for Dance (New York, N. Y.)—History.
I. Title.
GV1785.A1F693 2005
792.8'2 '0922—dc22
[B]   2004061158